P F

FINDING YOUR

Silver Lining

IN THE BUSINESS IMMIGRATION PROCESS

"Lauren's passion for educating and helping others comes through in her first book, where she focuses on showing readers how to find the 'Silver Lining,' even in the complex world of business immigration. It's a must read for anyone navigating the path to their American Dream."

—Mel Robbins, Best-selling Author, Speaker, and CNN Legal Analyst

"How do you take the complex and often complicated world of business immigration and make it rewarding, profitable and transformational? *Finding Your Silver Lining in the Business Immigration Process* is all that and more. Author and authority on business immigration, Lauren Cohen, has taken her years of wisdom and experience and is now sharing it on the pages of this life-changing book. For any business or person embarking on this adventurous road, this book is a MUST!"

—Allison Maslan, Best-selling Author, Business Coach, Speaker, contributor to *Entrepreneur* magazine, and CEO of Allison Maslan International

"It has been a pleasure to be a friend and mentor to Lauren and to watch her build her business as an immigration concierge. *Finding Your Silver Lining in the Business Immigration Process* is sure to 'wow' audiences with its sincerity, depth of information, and passion for making a difference—all great reflections of Lauren."

—Harvey Atkin, Renowned Actor, Comedian, Master of Ceremonies, and Philanthropist

"Lauren is a dedicated community activist, always willing to lend a hand to help, charitable in every way, and committed to making a difference in the lives of the people she touches. We look forward to Lauren sharing her expertise with our community and beyond."

—Danielle N. Hartman, MNM, CEO of Ruth & Norman Rales Jewish Family Services

"As a client, I can confirm that Lauren truly becomes a stakeholder and cares about simplifying the complicated business immigration process. By putting her carefully considered thoughts and approach into writing, *Finding Your Silver Lining in the Business Immigration Process* is sure to reflect the same level of care and commitment."

—Daniel Shields, J.D., M.B.A., President of AscendAmerica LLC

FINDING YOUR

IN THE BUSINESS IMMIGRATION PROCESS

AN INSIGHTFUL GUIDE TO IMMIGRANT & NON-IMMIGRANT BUSINESS VISAS

LAUREN A. COHEN, Esq.

Published by:
Silver Lining Publications
Boca Raton, Florida

This book contains general information about legal, business immigration, and related matters. This information is not intended to be exhaustive. It is not legal advice nor is it a substitute for legal advice and should not be treated or construed as such. It is not intended that readers rely on the information contained herein as an alternative to legal advice from an attorney or other professional legal services provider. The author and publisher are not responsible for any adverse effects or consequences resulting from the use of the information in this book. For specific questions about any legal, business immigration, or related matters, the author and publisher strongly suggest that readers consult an attorney or other professional services provider.

An independent compliance review of this guide has been performed by Margo Chernysheva, Esq. of MC Law Group.

ISBN-13: 978-0-69289-413-2

Interior and cover design: Gary A. Rosenberg

Printed in the United States of America

I dedicate this book to my amazing son,
Zevi Bryce Cohen, and his Zaidy,
my beloved dad, Allan Cohen,
of blessed memory.

Together, they were the inspiration for this
book and for the non-profit which this book
is helping to fund, Find My Silver Lining.

Contents

PART TWO: **IMMIGRANT VISAS**

Acknowledgments

I wish to thank the following people for their invaluable assistance with *Finding Your Silver Lining in the Business Immigration Process:*

Writer Patricia Nolan

Legal compliance editor and contributor of the Foreword to this book, Margo Chernysheva, Esq.

Editor Stacey Cohen, Esq.

Editor and writer Sharonne Edelman

Editor Angela Samay

To all of these wonderful people, and to everyone else who has seen me through this process—thank you for putting up with me!

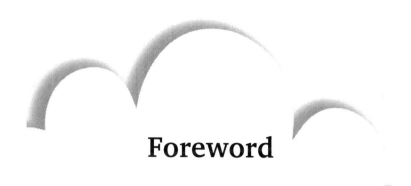

Foreword

The Complexity of the U.S. Immigration System

The U.S. immigration system is very complex, and navigating through it may often be an overwhelming task for the layperson. A certain level of expertise and know-how is required to successfully move through the process. Potential investors, individuals, and businesses seeking to immigrate to the United States are generally unfamiliar with the legal requirements, financial requirements, and government regulations that are all part of the process. It takes just one mistake or missed deadline to compromise the entire application process. A lot of this is avoidable by seeking the appropriate counsel from a team of qualified immigration experts.

The Importance of Seeking Proper Counsel

I often have clients who question the fact that since there is so much information available to the public, why is legal counsel needed? There are so many informational websites, online forums, blogs, and other platforms allegedly disseminating free advice and information, with many claiming to be experts in the field.

However, one should be careful not to jump to erroneous conclusions too quickly based on inaccurate or outdated information published online. Immigration laws and regulations are constantly changing and what you read online at any given point in time might already be out of date. In reality, the sheer volume of information available publicly can be more of a disservice than a benefit to the potential immigrant because that person has to carefully vet each piece of information found online or through *seemingly* reliable sources. Unfortunately, many potential immigrants are also victims of poor, unqualified allegedly *professional* advice or scam artists. This makes the process more time-consuming because the layperson has to navigate through a plethora of information and assess which sources are reliable.

Therefore, it is crucial that you seek true professional, qualified guidance to ensure that your application is successful. This will also save you considerable time and energy, and hence, money. It will also enable you to achieve your goals more expeditiously and, ultimately, to be successful. This is especially true since these matters concern the safety of both the individuals and their families.

Additionally, retaining proper counsel is the best way for you to ensure that you are pursuing the right type of visa. There are about a dozen of business visa categories with subcategories within those visas as well. Immigration counsel will help you determine which strategy is the most suited to your specific circumstances and can often research and offer potential visa solutions with which you are unfamiliar or that you thought were not even an option for you. The best immigration experts are those who can think outside of the box and find creative solutions to address your situation and help you achieve your immigration goals. In addition, qualified immigration attorneys have experience dealing with the immigration administration and know which options are more likely to be approved in which circumstances.

A Team of Multidisciplinary Experts Is a Must

Based on my own experience and from dealing with clients' past experiences (who were previously unrepresented), hiring a competent and experienced *team* of professionals specializing in business immigration cannot be overstated and is strongly recommended. This includes an experienced immigration attorney as well as a qualified business plan provider with experience developing business plans that meet the requirements of the United States Citizenship and Immigration Service (USCIS). Choosing an appropriate business and working with a business broker who understands the nuances of particular visas is also important, as is ensuring that the selected corporate attorney and CPA are cognizant of the specific requirements surrounding the visa being sought. A single-point-of-contact team to "quarterback" the entire application process is also highly recommended. This "quarterback" will oversee all project components, ensuring a pain-free, cost-effective, and ultimately successful experience.

A quarterback is even further essential in the complicated EB-5 process because a full spectrum of services and professionals are needed for approval, from conception of the project or business through its establishment and fulfillment of the complex range of EB-5 visa requirements. Working with an experienced quarterback eliminates the need to procure outside services from unrelated sources, which significantly streamlines the otherwise overwhelming process.

e-Council Inc. & MC Law Group

My law firm, MC Law Group,[1] started working with e-Council Inc., the principal of which is the author of this perceptive guide, Lauren Cohen, a few years ago. The collaboration has had a consistently positive impact on my clients' petitions and the number of approved applications. I soon recognized how important it is for my own immigration practice to work with a solid team of professionals, including financial advisors and business plan designers. It became abundantly clear that there is a significant difference in approval depending on the selected service providers as clients often insist on choosing based on price rather than quality, despite our recommendations. A strong team that produces quality work product is the key to success for any investor-type visa. Again, based on my own experience in dealing with

---

1. The experienced group of multilinguistic immigration attorneys at MC Law Group provide professional legal counsel to individuals and businesses on immigration and other legal matters with an international focus.

the immigration authorities, officers will look closely at the financials and one may be surprised at how thoroughly the administration delves into the business plans and financial viability of the projects, which are too often overlooked by the volume service providers.

e-Council Inc. serves attorneys and their clients as a duly qualified expert quarterback of all business immigration processes, as well as in a more supportive role as an immigration visa business plan company—the only company of its kind that was established and operated by attorneys to support other attorneys in their quest to secure business visas for their clients. It is a huge bonus to have the experts at e-Council Inc. available to analyze potential cases, consider the viability of success at the outset, and serve as a single-source, turnkey, concierge service assisting businesses seeking alternative capital from foreign investors as well as prospective immigrants to find their way to legal status in the United States.

—Margo Chernysheva, Esq.

Margo Chernysheva is the managing partner at MC Law Group and has extensive experience in the field of immigration law. She earned her undergraduate degree summa cum laude from Quinnipiac University, where she studied international business and economics. She worked as an executive in big pharmaceutical and small startup biotech companies for over ten years. She subsequently earned her law degree from the William S. Boyd School of Law at the University of Nevada, Las Vegas. She is admitted to practice law in Nevada and California and is fluent in English, French, Russian, and Armenian.

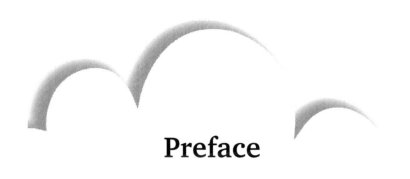

Preface

> *"Anyone who has never made a mistake*
> *has never tried anything new."*
>
> —ALBERT EINSTEIN, IMMIGRANT

The story behind this book involves a circuitous journey that begins with a dream—the American Dream to be specific.

Like the multitudes that came before me and have followed, I dreamed of immigrating to the United States in the pursuit of personal and professional happiness and success.

After earning my law degree from Osgoode Hall Law School in Toronto, Ontario, Canada, I realized that I wanted to pursue opportunities south of the border, so I consigned myself to the painstakingly long and taxing journey—both literally and figuratively—called the U.S. immigration process.

Unlike many applicants, I was fortunate. After years of (im)patiently waiting, my immigrant visa application was approved, and five years thereafter, in February 2012, I obtained my U.S. citizenship with my infant son in tow (he was fifteen months old). While I have now managed to begin turning my dream into a reality, and by doing so find my way into a new career and path, my journey was paved with a multitude of bumps and roadblocks. This is my story:

My first frustrating experience with the U.S. immigration process happened in 1997. I had been living and working legally in the United States in Florida as an in-house corporate attorney for a few years when I decided to take a trip to visit my family in Toronto. I had applied for an H1-B visa[1] and was awaiting approval from the United States Citizenship and Immigration Services (USCIS) at the time of the trip. Unbeknownst to me (having no experience with U.S. immigration law at the time), I technically had no standing as either a permanent or temporary U.S. resident because my visa was still in process. I did not know any better, and unfortunately I didn't bother to do the research. Hence, I was stuck in a bureaucratic limbo. As a result, shortly after my father dropped me off at the Toronto Pearson International Airport, the U.S. Customs and Border Protection (CBP) agents refused to let me pass (U.S. CBP is located in the Toronto Airport). CBP forced me to wait in a holding room while they questioned me and decided my fate.

After a stressful few hours, CBP released me, and my

---

1. An H-1B visa is a non-immigrant visa that allows U.S. companies to employ graduate-level staff in specialty occupations such as in law, technology, finance, medicine, etc. See Chapter 6 for more information.

father returned to retrieve me. As soon as I arrived at my parents' home, I called the USCIS Vermont Service Center, where my H-1B visa was being processed. I literally *begged* them to expedite my application so that I could return to my home and livelihood. Thankfully, as the terrible tragedy of 9/11 had yet to occur, and travel as well as immigration was not nearly as strict as it is today, I received a faxed copy of my Notice of Approval six hours later.

Within twenty-four hours of initially being detained, I managed to obtain temporary U.S. immigration status, rebook my flight, and was on a plane home. Note that this all happened nearly twenty years ago; this would *not* have been the case today—especially in terms of USCIS's ability and/or willingness to expedite the process.

I returned home with my temporary work visa and was ready to move forward with the process of obtaining a green card and permanent residency. While this experience would not be the last obstacle on my journey to permanent residency, it was my first step toward becoming an immigration attorney and the creation of e-Council Inc.

My company, e-Council Inc., was initially established as a business plan design and development company focused on startups and those seeking venture or angel capital,[2] but I soon discovered that most prospective clients did not have sufficient funds to pay for our services. e-Council Inc. then moved to the important

---

2. Angel capital is money invested by "angels"—that is, affluent investors—in startup or entrepreneurial endeavors, wherein the investor generally does not play an active role in the business.

business of serving other attorneys and their clients as an immigration visa business plan design and development company—the only company of its kind that was established and operated by attorneys to support other attorneys and their clients in their quest to secure various business immigration visas.

From there, e-Council expanded its scope of work and is now a single-source, turnkey, concierge service assisting businesses seeking alternative capital from foreign investors as well as prospective immigrants like myself to find their way to legal status in the United States without the headaches and hassles I had experienced.

The next bump in the road occurred a few years after the approval of my H1-B visa, and while it was truly devastating at the time, had I not experienced it, I doubt I would have ended up in the field of immigration law.

I had recently married a fellow Canadian who was also in the process of adjusting his immigrant status. We had been informed that once we were married, he would be entitled to derivative status as my spouse under my H1-B visa. My (now ex-) husband failed to disclose to me some circumstances related to his past in Canada that rendered him inadmissible in the eyes of USCIS. I did not find this out until we were returning home from our honeymoon in Thailand: we were connecting in Chicago O'Hare International Airport, and as we went through customs, I was shocked to find myself being escorted to a holding room once again. From there, my then-new husband was detained by U.S. CBP, expeditiously removed, then held in immigration jail, and subsequently deported back to Canada—all before my astonished eyes.

What CBP knew and of which I was unaware was that my ex-husband had a criminal record for which he received a pardon in Canada. At that time, USCIS did not recognize Canadian pardons. Therefore, my new spouse was inadmissible into the United States, even though, under normal circumstances, my H1-B visa should have applied to us both. I spent many difficult months after that horrible experience fighting with immigration attorneys on both sides of the border to overturn the deportation, so that my then-husband could return to the United States, but my efforts were unsuccessful. Ironically, during this challenging time, I received my own green card, and became a permanent U.S. resident.

As a last-ditch effort, I decided to go to Montreal to have my green card processed so that my spouse could attend the interview (since he was not permitted to enter the United States) with the goal that hopefully he would receive a "derivative" (spousal) green card. Unfortunately, his application was denied once again, while mine was processed without incident. The marriage was short-lived, and to be candid, the issues with admittance were but a small piece of the divorce puzzle.

Frustratingly enough, my run-ins with CBP were not the only obstacle I faced while making a home for myself in the United States. To make matters worse, I hit a few career-oriented roadblocks along the way as well. For example, I had initially immigrated to Florida in hopes of a fresh start while continuing to practice corporate law. While I did get a fresh start, my plan of practicing corporate law in the United States was hindered by restrictions set against me because I had attended law school in

Canada. Unfortunately, I discovered that I was unable to acquire a license to practice law within my home state of Florida without returning to school, which was simply not a viable option for me.

While I did obtain my Tennessee law license (many states, including Tennessee, recognize the equivalence of Canadian law degrees), I was still obstructed in my ability to find appropriate work and/or to pursue a suitable career path, since I was living and working in Florida. Unsure of how to pursue a career in my new home, many of the paths I tried resulted in dead ends, and I struggled to make ends meet. But I refused to give up. Eventually, after several false starts followed by a series of opportune events along with the help and advice of friends and colleagues, I found my place in the field of immigration law and started my current company, e-Council Inc., as I mentioned above.

It took a while for me to find my niche here in the United States, but when I finally did, it started with a business plan. A friend and colleague, who also happened to be a serial entrepreneur, reached out to me for help in writing a business plan for a new startup business. The combination made sense; as a corporate attorney and strong writer, I was equipped with the combination of knowledge and skill necessary to write a business plan— so I gave it a shot, and it proved successful.

The first plan led to a second, the second to a third, and so on until I was approached by my own immigration attorney, who, having heard about my business plan writing endeavors, asked for my assistance with writing a plan for a treaty investor non-immigrant business visa

(E-2). I tried my hand at this specialized business plan, and the visa petition was approved.

After the success of my first non-immigrant investor business plan, I started focusing entirely on writing business plans for non-immigrant business visas. In the beginning, I wrote plans only for E, L, and some H1-B visas, but eventually added EB-5 immigrant investor business plans to my repertoire, and over the years, my company has grown and transformed into the thriving turnkey full-service concierge business it is today. We have written in excess of 500 business plans for all types of immigrant and non-immigrant business visas, and have expanded our reach and scope of work well beyond the confines of our original focus on business plan writing.

So what started out as a one-woman company, initially focused on providing business plans for small businesses and those seeking immigration status, has transformed into a small, but thriving full-service concierge business immigration company, comprised of a handful of experts, who guide immigrant and non-immigrant investors, business owners, and project developers through the rough terrain that is the American business immigration process.

In my journey from corporate attorney to immigration lawyer and entrepreneur, I also secured my real estate license and ventured into the field of business brokerage. In so doing, I realized that there is a deficit of information available to those interested in the business immigration visa process, whether clients, their advisors and counsel, or others. What exists is either severely lacking or incredibly complicated.

From that realization, the idea for this book was born: a guidebook that explains the business immigration visa process in simple and easy terms, enabling those of us without a law degree to grasp complicated immigration concepts. This book was written with the intention of providing a supplement for professional support, not as a substitute for it. I cannot overemphasize the importance of proper, qualified legal counsel, and e-Council Inc. would be more than happy to work with you to coordinate such counsel.

I came to the United States in search of my version of the American Dream, and I found it in the form of paving a pathway for others to do the same. With my combined experience as an immigrant from Canada, a corporate lawyer, and a business plan designer, coupled with my business acumen and entrepreneurial spirit, I was able to facilitate the growth of my company into the flourishing business that it has become.

I refused to give up on my ideas or dreams, and I continue to push through every obstacle in the pursuit of my goals as I urge my clients and colleagues to do. Along with e-Council Inc., this book is the realization of my version of success by hopefully making the long and difficult process I went through much easier for those who follow after me, so that they too can realize their own version of what motivated me—the American Dream.

Just a few short weeks before submitting this guide to my editor, I set up a non-profit in Florida called Find My Silver Lining (www.findmysilverlining.com.) The non-profit was established in my father's memory. While some of the programming will be directly connected to my dad and my son and their relationship,[3] the overriding mission of the non-profit is for Find My Silver Lining to inspire and assist single mothers, working parents, and *mompreneurs* to focus on the bright side as they strive to lead fulfilling lives. The non-profit's goal is to help the target audience to have confidence and faith that there is indeed a silver lining for those of us who persevere and push through the clouds that are the tough times, ultimately to find their way to the silver lining.

I found my silver lining, and now I want you to help you find yours. I know in my heart that through my message and story, I can guide others to find theirs as well! Find My Silver Lining directly correlates to the purpose of the book, which is to help those seeking ways to access the United States through legal immigration, and to assist their legal and other counsel to access tools and information during the research process.

Business immigration can be complex and is often overwhelming. *Finding Your Silver Lining in the Business Immigration Process* serves to facilitate the process wherever possible. It will function as a springboard to your broader immigration plan, which should definitely include qualified immigration attorneys, accountants, professional business plan writers, and other stakeholders and trusted advisors.

---

3. Though not directly related to the topic of this book, Find My Silver Lining is also funding a program through Jewish Family Services in memory of my beloved father, Allan Cohen, of blessed memory, the focus of which is to match children without grandfathers/grandparents to grandfathers/grandparents wishing to be meaningfully involved in the children's lives.

Introduction

"Give me your tired, your poor, your huddled masses yearning to breathe free, the wretched refuse of your teeming shore. Send these, the homeless, tempest-tossed to me, I lift my lamp beside the golden door!"

—STATUE OF LIBERTY PLAQUE

As one of the most recognizable landmarks in the world, the Statue of Liberty represents the promise of the American Dream to many all over the world. When we think of U.S. immigration, the image of Lady Liberty holding her torch is an undeniably powerful one. But when the huddled masses referenced in the famous poem arrived in the United States, the federal government had not yet established or funded a dedicated agency tasked with handling their entry in any systematic way. What we know today as the United States Citizenship and Immigration Services (USCIS) began as a very small part of the Treasury Department and evolved over time, reflecting not only the sheer volume of immigrants

1

entering the United States but also historical events and the fluctuating attitudes of American society.

The main draw of the United States has always been labor. The chance to find employment and make a decent living has pushed many people to leave their native land and travel to the "new" world. Throughout history, employers' need for labor (often inexpensive labor) has inspired lenient legislation and encouragement of immigration. But labor has not been the only catalyst. Escape from persecution of every kind has also inspired many to make the journey. And, of course, there have been immigrants who came to the United States against their will and in chains. Whatever the reason, immigrants have had a profound impact on every aspect of American life, and the laws that have been enacted to regulate their entry, status, and rights run the gamut of well-meaning to outrageous.

A BRIEF HISTORY OF AMERICAN IMMIGRATION AND IMMIGRATION LAWS

From the eighteenth century to the present day, immigration into the United States has changed and evolved with each new law and regulation enacted. In this section, we will take a look at some of the more meaningful developments over our history.

18th-Century America

When the United States won the Revolutionary War (the American War of Independence), it encouraged immigration to fill the labor needs of a growing nation. The only formal law of note was the Naturalization Act of 1790, which essentially defined who could become an American citizen. Reflective of the beliefs and values of the time, this Act stipulated that only free white persons could become citizens. And while white women were allowed to become citizens, they could exercise very few of the rights of citizenship that are enjoyed today, such as voting, owning land, and inheriting property. Things would begin to change by the mid-nineteenth century when the burden of immigration regulation gradually shifted from the states to the federal government.

19th-Century Changes

The 1800s saw steadily increasing immigration to the United States, as well as the emergence of waves of collective fear and distrust of immigrants, propelling federal regulations that reflected anti-immigrant sentiments. These laws and regulations continued throughout the twentieth century, but still, those who wanted to come to the United States found a way, either legally or illegally, as is the case today.

Some noteworthy events characterize nineteenth-century immigration patterns. In the late 1840s, the Irish Potato Famine pushed more than 600,000 men, women, and children out of Ireland and into the United States. They generally settled in the larger cities nearby ports of entry and often worked in unskilled jobs. They faced discrimination and prejudice but were able to assimilate successfully over time, even after the Civil War when they competed for jobs with the newly freed African Americans. Millions of German immigrants also came to the United States during the mid-nineteenth century, mostly settling in the Midwest as farmers and successfully integrating into American culture.

With the job opportunities presented by westward expansion and the Industrial Revolution, it seemed that despite some flickers of social unrest, America would continue to welcome immigrants.

This changed with the Chinese Exclusion Act (1882) and the 1885 Alien Contract Labor law and 1887 amendment, which were enacted in response to the large numbers of Asian immigrants who entered California as a result of the gold rush. The Chinese Exclusion Act essentially stopped the immigration of Chinese workers. Only domestic servants and diplomats were allowed to enter the United States. Further, a class of approximately 100,000 Chinese permanent residents was created. These people, already in the United States, were not allowed to become American citizens, and if they left for any reason, they would not be allowed reentry. The 1885 Alien Contract Labor Law and its amendment in 1887 went a step further and stopped contract labor of immigrants from any country.

No recruiting of immigrants with the promise of work was allowed. This especially targeted unskilled laborers, particularly Chinese and Irish laborers, who often came to the United States under contract or as indentured servants. This law and its amendment were discriminatory in many ways, especially in their exemptions. Workers with special skills that were in short supply in the United States were welcome, as were those who could pay their own passage. These laws were specifically aimed at working-class immigrants. They were harsh and exclusionary, and were the first on the books that sought to restrict immigration specifically by nationality and economic class.

The federal government gave in to pressure from Californians after the heyday of the gold rush and the building of the railroads, who felt a threat to U.S. wages by immigrants willing to work for less pay. But the same entry restrictions did not apply to Asian merchants or students, only to laborers. In 1903, the U.S. government expanded the list of those who were restricted from immigrating to include those who had been convicted of crimes of moral turpitude (behavior collectively frowned upon by a community), those with contagious diseases, and polygamists. It was clear by the beginning of the twentieth century that the changes and new immigration restrictions would require an agency that could enforce them.

In addition, the definition of citizenship changed after the Civil War, with the 14th Amendment to the U.S. Constitution. This amendment granted citizenship to all native-born Americans (to include newly freed slaves), but the process of naturalization for those born outside the United States was largely left to each of the nation's more than 5,000 naturalization courts. There was no consistency regarding requirements, fees, or process, and the need for federal oversight of naturalization was recommended for uniformity and enforcement.

20th-Century Reform

The twentieth century saw the continued surge of immigrants to the United States by the millions (nearly 15,000,000) between 1900 and 1920. These numbers are hard to imagine today in such a short space of time, especially considering that immigration from Europe decreased greatly during the carnage of World War I (1914–1918). The changes to American society, especially in urban areas, were profound. Different languages, cultures, religious beliefs, and customs flooded into the country. The U.S. attitude toward immigration would fluctuate between openness and fear; even a presidential commission was formed to understand the conditions that were pushing this massive number of immigrants to U.S. shores. Conditions, once they arrived, were also studied, and although in certain cases abysmal, they still perceived them as better than what they left behind. Another notable twentieth-century immigration development was the overhaul of the relatively unchecked border crossings between Canada and Mexico with the Presidential Proclamation of August 8, 1918, requiring passports and the issuance of Border Crossing Cards.

The 1920s emerged as the decade that placed the most dramatic restrictions on immigration, putting into law the first quotas. The 1921 Emergency Quota Act was strictly enforced and immigration dropped from 800,000 to 300,000 in one year. These quotas were tightened in 1924, and the U.S. Border Patrol was established, foreshadowing the issues and tension that exist today between the United States and Mexico.

The term "alien" as a legal term to describe immigrants was coined in 1937, and the obsession with criminal or "illegal aliens" became the focus of enforcement. Interestingly, while on the one hand encouraging Mexican immigration to the American southwest to fill low-paying agricultural jobs in the forties and fifties, the U.S. government on the other hand implemented the offensive Operation Wetback in 1954, with a view to catching undocumented Mexican immigrants and deporting them. It was understandably very unpopular with Mexican-Americans and fell apart due to lack of resources to enforce it.

World War II Effect

With the advent of another world war, on the heels of a devastating economic depression, U.S. immigration experienced another ebb. This was reminiscent of the dip that happened during World War I. Bloodshed was happening in Europe at the hands of the Nazis, and their allies—the Japanese—ensured that the United States would get involved in the fighting by attacking Pearl Harbor in 1941. What followed was more loss of life as well as the austerity and sacrifice that war demands. The U.S. government responded to the conflict by requiring Italian Americans and German Americans to register and stripping Japanese Americans of their freedoms by putting them in internment camps. The perceived security threat of these immigrant groups was fueled by a collective mistrust and the extreme stress of war.

All of this work registering aliens, managing internment camps, and increasing border security meant the

Immigration and Naturalization Service (INS) was busier than ever. It increased its staff from 4,000 to 8,000 to cope. Unfortunately, the United States did not respond effectively to the plight of Jews fleeing Nazi persecution. The existing quotas were strictly enforced, and these refugees were not given the safe haven they so desperately needed, despite the fact that details of German plans for Jewish extermination had reached American shores. After the war, the United States did accept some Jewish refugees who had survived Nazi persecution, but they were by no means welcomed with open arms or in huge numbers. World War II, along with being so horrific and brutal, was not the U.S. immigration policy's shining moment either.

Post-War Flow

Finally, in 1965, the Hart-Celler Act did away with quotas and racial barriers to citizenship, and the INS sought to reasonably regulate entry and citizenship and encourage immigrants with special skills and relatives already in the United States. The Hart-Celler Act paved the way for the Immigration Act of 1990, upon which so much of this book is based, defining opportunities for foreign nationals to come to the United States to start businesses and contribute to the U.S. economy with their skills and expertise. With the Immigration Act of 1990, legal immigration increased by 40 percent, and while there were still challenges at our southern border, the patterns of immigration seemed to settle into a manageable flow.

Post 9/11 Emphasis

The tragic events of September 11, 2001, forever changed the way the United States controls its borders, with a new emphasis on national security and the identification and removal of criminal aliens and terrorists. The disbanded INS was replaced on March 1, 2003, with the U.S. Citizenship and Immigration Services (USCIS), one of three agencies under the Department of Homeland Security (DHS). The other two agencies are Immigration and Customs Enforcement (ICE), which specifically oversees immigration enforcement (that is, enforcement of applicable immigration laws) and Customs and Border Protection (CBP) for enhanced border security. All three agencies work closely together to protect our borders, enforce current immigration laws, and identify and remove criminal aliens/terrorists and security threats.

While this book focuses on business visas, it is necessary to understand immigration history in the United States and observe the events and trends that have shaped our current laws. Immigration history is indeed the history of this country, and despite the many challenges faced and missteps government agencies have made along the way, Lady Liberty beckons, and there is still a strong desire around the world to come to the United States and have a chance to pursue the American Dream.

BUSINESS IMMIGRATION OVERVIEW

There is no doubt that business immigration programs in the United States are complex and competitive, necessitating a level of expertise to successfully negotiate the multitude of processes. Potential immigrants and investors are often unfamiliar with the legal rules, financial requirements, and government regulations that comprise the process. It takes just one mistake, omission, or missed deadline—much of which is avoidable—to derail the entire application process, resulting in delays in the immigration timeline or, worse, denials.

Despite these challenges, many domestic business immigration programs are incredibly popular, and with good reason. Foreign nationals who are eager to participate in and contribute to the American economy while gaining the right to a non-immigrant visa, permanent resident green card, and/or other options are expressing interest in, and applying for, these programs.

Opportunity is a great motivator—but without the know-how of where to start, prospective immigrants will no doubt waste time, energy, and money chasing the *wrong* type of visa. There are numerous cases of people who were doing just that, diligently trying their best to complete and submit the *wrong application* or to engage in the *wrong business* or to make the *wrong investment* – and all too often to also hire the *wrong professionals*. For this and many other reasons, although this guide will provide significant invaluable resources and information, retaining experienced, qualified counsel cannot be overstated and is <u>strongly</u> recommended!

CHAPTER 1

Business Visas General Overview: Immigrant versus Non-immigrant

*"The American Dream is that dream of a
land in which life should be better and richer
and fuller for everyone, with opportunity for
each according to ability or achievement."*

—JAMES TRUSLOW ADAMS, HISTORIAN

The U.S. immigration process is an incredibly complex and often daunting experience for those who dare apply. Potential U.S. immigrants face many obstacles— poor professional advice, scam artists and fraudulent investment opportunities coupled with legal limitations, visa quotas and a wide range of other restrictions—in their journey toward living and working in the United States. These impediments are often time-consuming, expensive, and can even be detrimental to the immigration application. Hiring a competent and experienced team of qualified professionals is crucial to the application's ultimate success.

As noted earlier, the purpose of this book is to act as a general guide to set you on the correct path toward procuring the most suitable business visa for your circumstances. People who pursue the immigration process are unique individuals (and families) with a myriad of conditions behind their reasons for choosing to immigrate. To keep things light, this book is written from a "one-size-fits-all" perspective, and should **not** *be used in lieu of professional counsel.* The intent of this book is to provide you with some basic knowledge to begin your journey. When finished, you will set this book down with a better understanding of the available business visa options, for which visa(s) you best qualify, and an idea of what will need to be submitted with the visa application, as well as the professionals you will need to hire.

The first step in this process is figuring out which visa best applies to each unique situation, and then to hire a qualified business immigration attorney to help make this choice and then to pursue it. It is commonly said that knowledge is power, and in the case of business visas, knowledge definitely affords prospective immigrants to feel empowered. However, the available information, especially on the Internet, is multifaceted, complicated, and confusing, and can often lead to information overload—overwhelming those who did not go to law school and have a harder time interpreting the data. Thus, it is recommended to use this guide to help with grasping the basics while seeking counsel from qualified attorneys who live and breathe business immigration every day, helping clients successfully wade through the murky waters.

There are a multitude of business visa options available, some of which are not covered in this guide. While I cannot outline every single possible visa opportunity,

I can outline and you can examine some of the most popular and effectual prospective immigrant and non-immigrant visas. It should be noted that there are not only dozens of business visa categories but subcate-gories within those visas as well.

When determining the best business visa for which to apply, it is also essential to know the difference between an immigrant and non-immigrant visa, and the impact of each on the applicants. An immigrant visa is one that leads directly to permanent residency and eventually to an opportunity to apply for U.S. citizenship after the required time has lapsed following the granting of legal permanent residence. A non-immigrant visa is temporary in nature and allows qualified applicants (and their immediate families) to live and work in the United States for a limited duration. Some temporary work visas, such as the L-1A or H-1B visas, can be converted to immigrant visas for qualified applicants, should the need arise.

Many who are desirous of living and working in the United States are under the impression that they need to apply for an immigrant visa in order to do so, and this is simply not the case. While immigrant visas do allow immigrants to live and work in the United States, they are intended specifically for those who wish to gain U.S. residency (otherwise known as legal permanent

---

1. American Immigration Center. "Differences Between Immigrant Visas and Non-Immigrant Visas." Accessed March 30, 2017. www.us-immigration.com/blog/differences-between-immigrant-visas -and-non-immigrant-visas.

residency or a green card).[1] There are many benefits to taking the immigrant visa path from the get-go, such as receiving almost the same rights and protections as natural-born Americans upon application success, but there are downsides as well. For instance, the process is usually lengthy and commands additional costs and professional support.[2]

There are five types of immigrant application processes options to choose from—EB-1, EB-2, EB-3, EB-4, and EB-5, which are collectively restricted to roughly 140,000 total visas available each year, as of the time of this writing.[3] This is important to consider when choosing the appropriate visa, as the quotas placed on immigrant visas severely limit the number of aliens allowed to immigrate to the United States each year, and can cause further delays in the application process. For instance, if the quotas are met before the application has been received, then the applicant(s) will have to wait until the next fiscal year (or even longer if there is a heavy backlog of applications).

Non-immigrant visas are a great alternative to immigrant visas, and can often be transitioned to an immigrant visa and permanent residency. There are over twenty non-immigrant visa options available—issued for the purposes of business or pleasure.[4] For example, the

2. Berkeley International Office. "Non-immigrant vs. Immigrant Status." UC Berkeley. Accessed March 30, 2017. international office.berkeley.edu/non-immigrant_vs_immigrant.

3. U.S. Citizenship and Immigration Services. "Permanent Workers." USCIS. Accessed March 30, 2017. www.uscis.gov/working-united -states/permanent-workers.

B-1 and B-2 visas are distributed specifically for travel, but unlike other travel visas, the B-1 allows the holder to work in the United States temporarily for a maximum of six months (in many cases investigating business opportunities for the future). Temporary work visas, like the H1-B visa, which I held when I first moved to the United States, or L-1B (specialized knowledge intracompany transferee), can be renewed, as long as certain criteria have been met for a set period of time. Additionally, after being granted a non-immigrant temporary work visa, such as the aforementioned H1-B and L-1B, aliens have the opportunity to settle in to their new lives in the United States, start the lengthy application process for permanent residency, and continue to live and work in the United States while they await approval from USCIS. Another benefit to applying for a non-immigrant temporary work visa is that while some are subject to limits on the number of visas issued each fiscal year, such as the H1-B visa which is capped at 65,000 visas distributed per year, many, such as the L-1 visas, have no annual quotas placed on them restricting the number of available visas.[5]

Whether or not attaining U.S. citizenship is the end goal of your migration journey, both immigrant and non-immigrant visas have their own unique advantages. What is truly important when determining the best visa

4. McFayden, Jennifer. "What Is the Difference Between an Immigrant Visa and a Non-immigrant Visa?" ThoughtCo. Accessed March 30, 2017. immigration.about.com/od/usvisas/f/VisaTypeFAQ.htm.

5. Immigralaw. "Visa Quota Chart." Accessed March 30, 2017. www.immigralaw.com/english/immigrationquotas.html.

to pursue is which available option best suits your current wants and needs. No matter which route you choose, this journey is both time-consuming and expensive. Before moving forward, it is crucial to review your reasons for taking this journey. Ask yourself a few questions and define your goals:

- What are your end goals for this journey?

- How much time are you willing or able to invest in achieving your goals?

- How much money are you willing or able to invest in achieving your goals?

- What brought you here, to this moment, reading this book?

- Are you ready?

- Is it worth it?

Once you have figured out your answers to the questions above, you will be ready to move forward to figure out the best option for your path to the United States. While I cannot guarantee that reading this book will prevent every possible bump in the road, I can promise that this book will arm you with the general knowledge needed to move forward with the confidence that the journey will end in success. My goal is to help prevent you from experiencing any unnecessary setbacks and headaches, and to leave you with the wisdom and wherewithal to power through any obstacle set in your path.

This guide is divided into two parts—Part One covers non-immigrant visas and Part Two is dedicated to immigrant visas, with each following chapter dedicated solely to one type of business visa. Most chapters also include sections that address real-life scenarios and frequently asked questions (FAQs). The information included herein will assist you in determining which of these visas *might* suit your circumstances, so that you can be well-equipped to consult with appropriate immigration counsel and other trusted advisors on your path to achieving your own American Dream.

Please remember, however that this guide is *not* intended to replace legal advice and should not be relied upon as such. Please consult with e-Council Inc. or a qualified attorney to discuss your circumstances and to decide upon the best course of action to pursue.

PART ONE

Non-immigrant Visas

*"I never dreamed about success.
I worked for it."*

—Estée Lauder,
CHILD OF IMMIGRANTS

CHAPTER 2

L-1 Visas
(Intracompany Transfers)

*"Everywhere immigrants have enriched and
strengthened the fabric of American life."*

—JOHN F. KENNEDY,
35TH PRESIDENT OF THE UNITED STATES

A good place to begin a discussion of business based non-immigrant visas is with the L-1 Intracompany Transfer visas. These visas are geared toward foreign companies wishing to transfer an executive, manager (L-1A), or specialized knowledge employee (L-1B) to live and work in the United States in one of those capacities. They are valuable tools for multinational companies and companies wishing to expand their operations in the United States or open a U.S. branch or office. L-1 visas are non-immigrant visas, but they are considered "dual intent," meaning that there is a path to permanent residence available to L-1 visa holders.

Prior to the 1970s, it was difficult for U.S. companies with offices abroad to transfer highly skilled and trained employees from a foreign branch to a U.S. office. To rectify this issue, Congress created the L-1 visa category, enabling U.S. entities with foreign offices to temporarily transfer an executive, manager, or employee with specialized knowledge to a U.S. office from abroad. This visa was also available for the transfer of a qualified executive, manager, or employee to open a new U.S. branch or office.

Since the 1970s Congress has modified the L-1 visa two additional times. The first time, in 1990, the visa was split into two categories; the L-1A for executives and managers and the L-1B for employees with specialized knowledge. This modification also broadened the definition of "manager" and "specialized knowledge," set the current limits on the allotted period of stay, and turned the visa category into a dual-intent visa.

The second modification came in 2004, with the L-1 Visa Reform Act. This Act sought to ensure that the L-1B specialized workers were working primarily for the U.S. company that petitioned on their behalf and not for an "unaffiliated" company. This is important because one of the strictest requirements of the L-1 visa category is the clear establishment of a "qualified relationship" between the U.S. company petitioner and its foreign entity. Under this reform act, companies were not allowed to import foreign workers and contract them out to clients or other unaffiliated companies. The reform act also added an additional fee to the application process, on top of the existing fees. This $500 fee was dubbed an "anti-fraud" or "fraud-detection" fee.

Who Can Petition for an L-1 Employee?
(Qualifying Entities)

An individual cannot apply for L-1 status, but rather the U.S. entity must apply on behalf of the proposed beneficiary. This U.S. entity petitioning for the foreign national and the foreign entity where the foreign national has been employed must either be the same company, part of the same company, or be related (parent, branch, affiliate, or subsidiary). If the affiliation cannot be proven with tax records, websites, organizational documents, or other similar proof, then the executive, manager, or employee is ineligible to receive an L-1 visa. The following are some useful definitions for this determination:

- A *parent company* is defined as a majority owner of the other organization (either a subsidiary or affiliate). The parent company can either be the U.S. or foreign entity.

- A *branch office* is defined as a fully functioning office of the same company that conducts real business in a separate location—i.e., a U.S. company with a branch office in a foreign country (or vice versa).

- A *subsidiary* is defined as an organization that is controlled by a *parent company.*

- An *affiliate* is defined as one of two *subsidiaries* or legal entities, which are both owned and/or controlled by the same *parent company,* individual, or group of individuals.

- The U.S. company name is substantially similar to the parent company.

- The U.S. company ownership is substantially similar to the parent company.

Other L-1 Visa Requirements

Once a qualifying relationship between the U.S. entity and foreign entity has been established, there are other requirements to consider. The L-1 visa beneficiary must be transferred to the U.S. to provide the same or similar executive, managerial, or specialized knowledge services that he/she provided the foreign entity.

The U.S. organization must be currently conducting business as an employer in both the U.S. and one other country for the duration of the visa beneficiary's stay in the United States. If the foreign national is coming to the United States to open a new branch office of this company, an exception can be made. However, the foreign national charged with opening the new branch office must have it up and running within one year of arrival.

Finally, to qualify for an L-1 visa, the foreign national must have been employed by the qualifying foreign entity for at least twelve continuous months within the three years prior to entering the United States. Their employment must have been full-time in nature as well as in an executive, managerial, or specialized knowledge capacity.

Executive, Manager, and Specialized Knowledge Worker

USCIS has specific definitions of an executive, manager, and specialized knowledge worker's duties and qualifications. These definitions go beyond common knowledge and set a high standard for a potential L-1 visa beneficiary.

L-1A Executive—an L-1A qualifying executive must make important decisions without much oversight. This discretionary decision-making must include company goal-setting and policy-making. An L-1A executive must direct the management of the company. Having a title is not enough. A detailed list of duties, including percentages for each duty, should be furnished at the time of the application submission. Keep in mind that USCIS may scrutinize the company itself to make sure that the U.S. business appears to require an executive to run efficiently. In the case of an L-1A executive, the size and revenue of the company matter.

L-1A Manager—as with the L-1A executive, the title of manager is not enough to qualify an applicant. The duties of the L-1A manager will be reviewed carefully. It is not sufficient that the manager will have a staff that he/she supervises. Supervision of other employees is of course a managerial function, but an L-1A manager must also prove that his/her management is essential to the proper functioning of the company. The budget that an L-1A managerial applicant controls will be a consideration, as will the scope of his/her authority and the nature of the business itself.

L-1B Specialized Knowledge Employee—this classification may very well be the most regulated of the L-1 classifications, requiring only key employees to be eligible for L-1B visa consideration. To have specialized knowledge, the foreign national must be able to prove an advanced understanding of the company, including its processes and, if applicable, its products. A specialized knowledge employee must be able to transfer that knowledge abroad, and therefore have an understanding of global markets. A petitioning employer must prove that not having this specialized knowledge worker in the United States and having to train someone else to do this job would cause a significant hiccup in the functioning of the U.S. employer.

In the case of all L-1 visa applicants, the foreign company that is opening a new branch/office must be able to prove that it can afford to hire these executives, managers, or specialized knowledge employees; that it has secured a physical premises adequate for the beneficiaries and others to work (working from home is not permitted); and that it has adequate capital to begin operations (i.e., offering goods or services for sale) in the United States.

L-1 Visa Length of Stay

L-1A visa holders can live and work in the United States in this status for a *maximum* of seven years. If the beneficiary arrives in the United States to work for an established branch, subsidiary, or affiliate, his/her initial visa is good for three years and can be renewed in two-year increments until the maximum of seven years is reached.

For L-1A visa holders coming to the United States to open a new branch or office, an initial one-year visa is granted. The beneficiary can again extend the visa in two-year increments until the seven years maximum is reached. After that initial year, the business being run will be reviewed to make sure it is a viable business providing goods and/or services for profit. It doesn't have to be a hugely successful branch that first year, but it must prove its viability.

The maximum length of stay for an L-1B visa holder is five years. As with the L-1A new branch/office requirement, an L-1B visa holder designated to work in a new branch/office is granted an initial one-year visa. The viability of the business will be assessed after that first year, and if the evidence is satisfactory, USCIS will grant extensions in two-year increments until the maximum of five years has been reached. For all other L-1B visa holders, the initial approval is for three years, allowing for one two-year extension.

Families of L-1 Visa Beneficiaries

One of the benefits of applying for an L-1 visa is that upon arrival in the United States, an L-1 visa beneficiary's spouse can apply for a social security number and work authorization, and his/her children (under age 21) can attend school (but not work) while in the United States. The L-1 spouse (L-2) can apply for work authorization on an as-needed basis.

Applying for an L-1 Visa

The L-1 visa application process involves the filing of an I-129 petition for a Non-immigrant Worker with the accompanying L Supplement. This petition must be submitted to USCIS with the appropriate fee and supporting documentation. The fee at the time of this writing is $460, but fees change periodically, so it is always a good idea to visit the USCIS website (https://www.uscis.gov/forms/our-fees) to check the latest fee schedule. The additional current $500 fraud prevention and detection fee must also be included. If an employer petitioner seeks premium (or expedited) processing, an additional $1,225 should be submitted. The supporting documentation required includes:

- A letter from the U.S. employer confirming that the L-1 beneficiary will be employed by them in a qualified capacity in the United States;

- Additional evidence of ownership, such as tax returns and records of stock ownership;

- A customized business plan detailing the business model, business goals and projections for the U.S. business;

- Documentation evidencing a qualifying relationship between the U.S. and foreign business entities, such as a statement by an authorized official describing relationship of ownership and control between the companies (explanation included in the business plan);

- Financial viability, if the beneficiary is entering the United States to establish a new office or branch (included in the business plan);

- Company's organizational chart (included in the business plan);

- Employee's resume and detailed job description (details included in the business plan);

- Documentation that shows the relationship between the parent company and its subsidiaries, such as Securities and Exchange Commission (SEC) filings; and

- A letter signed by an authorized official detailing the employee's qualifications to work in the United States in a managerial, executive, or specialized knowledge capacity. This includes the job duties, level of authority, as well as salary and dates of employment with the foreign entity.

If the application is successful, an L-1 beneficiary currently in the United States in another lawful status can change his/her status to L-1 without leaving the country. Please note, those who entered the United States on ESTA (Electronic System for Travel Authorization) are not eligible to change status in the United States. USCIS issues an I-797 (Notice of Action), which is a notice confirming that the applicant's L petition has been approved. This form is attached to the applicant's departure/entry record (I-94) and his/her status as an L-1 is affirmed.

If an applicant is living outside of the United States, he/she must make an appointment with an embassy or consulate in his/her home nation and bring the I-797 approval notice to the appointment. This can cause additional waiting time because of the appointment requirement. Some embassies/consulates do not have any interview openings for several weeks, which can be frustrating to the L-1 beneficiary eager to begin working in the United States. In addition, the consulate/embassy has the power to review and scrutinize supporting documentation to determine the validity of the L-1 petition. This can result in additional stress and delay. In some cases, even an approved I-129 did not stop a consulate from denying the actual visa to a prospective L-1 visa application based on the consular officer's discretion. However, if the application procedure is followed carefully and the supporting documentation is compelling, the L-1 beneficiary will be able to enter the United States and begin to work.

Blanket L-1 Petitions

The blanket L-1 petition program is beneficial for larger international employers engaging in commercial trade or services and allows multiple L-1 beneficiaries to enter the United States. If an L-1 blanket petition is approved, the petitioning U.S. employer doesn't have to prove its qualifying relationship with the foreign employer for each individual L-1 petition. An approved blanket L-1 makes for much faster processing of applicants and issuance of visas. The criteria for a blanket L-1 petition to be successful includes the number of L-1 petitions filed in the past year, the number of foreign offices/branches/subsidiaries the U.S. employer has, revenue, and number of U.S. workers.

TABLE 2.1. 2015 L VISAS ISSUED

L-1	78,537
L-2	86,067
Total	164,604

TABLE 2.2. 2015 L VISA DISTRIBUTION BY COUNTRY

COUNTRY	NUMBER OF L VISAS	COUNTRY	NUMBER OF L VISAS
Argentina	1,509	Japan	10,343
Australia	2,685	Kazakhstan	2,364
Brazil	7,557	Mexico	10,772
China Mainland	10,258	Netherlands	1,965
Colombia	1,123	Philippines	1,770
France	5,751	Russia	2,233
Germany	4,503	South Africa	1,517
Great Britain and Northern Ireland	10,742	South Korea	4,580
		Spain	2,680
India	52,790	Sweden	1,237
Israel	2,507	Ukraine	1,147
Italy	1,513	Venezuela	1,971

The Path to Permanent Residence

For the L-1A executive or manager who decides to stay in the United States, the path to permanent residence can be relatively straightforward. The best course of action is to apply for an employment-based green card, and in the case of an L-1A, the best option is the EB-1C or Priority Workers: Multinational Executives and Managers visa.

The EB-1C visa has similar requirements to the L-1A visa; most importantly, it allows the L-1A applicants to skip the Permanent Labor Certification program, more commonly referred to as "PERM" (PERM is a time-consuming and expensive process used to determine whether there is a qualified U.S. worker available for the position the foreign national holds and is seeking to retain permanently; it will be discussed in greater detail in Part Two). It is a requirement for many of the employment-based green card applicants, and if it can be avoided, time, monetary expenditure, and stress can also be minimized.

As with the L-1 visa application process, the beneficiary's employer must petition USCIS, but this time using a Form I-140 (Immigrant Petition for Alien Worker) along with Form I-485 (Application to Register Permanent Residence or Adjust Status). The process usually takes about a year, and, ideally, the petition should be filed at least a year prior to the expiration of the L-1A visa. Dependents are also eligible to receive green cards through this process.

For the L-1B visa holder, the path to permanent residence is not as straightforward. Unfortunately, there is no way to avoid PERM, and L-1B's must endure the same lengthy process as some of the other employment-based green card applicants. This process can take up to several years to complete and is subject to annual quotas that are limited by both the employment-based visa category, as well the applicant's country of birth. The path to permanent residence may take longer, but it is possible. If the application is ultimately successful, an I-140 petition as well as an I-485 petition can be filed, and the L-1B visa holder and his/her family can receive permanent green cards.

The Benefits of L-1

There is no doubt that the L-1 option is an attractive one for professionals hoping to come to the United States to live and work. A number of benefits make it particularly attractive for petitioning employers:

- L-1 visas offer an option for the transfer of qualified employees from a foreign entity to its U.S. counterpart to expand its business or establish a new branch or office.

- L-1 visas are not subject to quotas or limits on the number issued by USCIS (unlike other non-immigrant visas such as the H-1B).

- L-1 visas increase the international competitiveness of multinational companies based in the United States.

- L-1 dependents have the benefit of working and attending school while in the United States.

- L-1A beneficiaries can transition from non-immigrant status to immigrant status through the EB-1C visa (avoiding PERM).

- L-1B beneficiaries can transition from non-immigrant to immigrant status through any of the employment-based green card visa options.

Some L-1 Disadvantages

Although the L-1 application process is straightforward, because of fraud, scrutiny by USCIS and embassy/consular adjudicators has increased in the last decade and the documentation provided must be strong and compelling. If not, the application will be subject to a Request for Evidence (RFE), which causes delays and frustration. Almost 50 percent of L-1 visa applications are subject to RFEs, and 35 percent are ultimately denied, so this visa is not without its challenges.

The additional anti-fraud fee of $500 was added to existing filing fees for a reason. There was a trend of dishonesty, fake documents, and shell companies[1] that raised the scrutiny bar (and the cost) for all potential L-1 beneficiaries.

As with all other immigration-related topics, there is controversy. Critics argue that jobs are being taken away from qualified U.S. workers and wages are not protected because the L-1 visa is not subject to wage requirements. The fraud perpetrated by unscrupulous companies (fake documents, shell companies) and the tendency of some organizations to have a workforce made up of 50 percent

---

1. Essentially, shell companies are dormant entities that are used to manipulate situations to accomplish certain goals, such as raising capital, that may not be available to startup or similar entities.

foreign nationals have inspired not only criticism, but also increased scrutiny by USCIS and other government agencies tasked with controlling foreign labor in the United States.

Despite the challenges, the L-1 visa is a solid option for companies seeking to expand business in the United States and for foreign nationals hoping to bring their professional skills to the U.S. workforce, particularly if the beneficiary wishes to ultimately pursue permanent residence.

REAL-LIFE L-1 SCENARIOS

Scenario 1

The president of Pop Fizz Cola, a popular soft drink in Colombia, is seeking to open a branch in the United States, specifically South Florida, where the Latin population is significant. To do that, she needs a small team to go with her to ensure its success. She needs to bankroll the endeavor as well as set the branch goals, monitor progress, and lead all aspects of the operation. She also needs to bring her marketing manager with her in order to have the best chance at success in bringing this soft drink to a new market. The third member of her team is a longtime employee of Pop Fizz who knows the ins and outs of the company, and more important, is an expert in the Pop Fizz recipe and its quality control.

The president will hire local workers as general office staff, distributors, etc., but the two employees from Colombia are essential to the opening of this new branch.

Pop Fizz files an L-1A petition for the president and her marketing manager and an L-1B for the employee in charge of the soft drink production. They seek premium processing. The petitions are approved within a matter of weeks after submitting the necessary documentation, and the L-1 visa is issued for an initial period of one year. The employees will be eligible to extend their visas if they can prove after that year that the branch is a success or on its way to becoming a viable independent branch.

Scenario 2

A multinational IT company is hoping to transfer an employee from England to the United States to grow one of its subsidiaries. This employee has been a functional manager with this company for several years and has been entrusted with growing other offices in various places around the UK as well as Australia and Canada. She has extensive experience and a natural talent for growing a business and her track record is impressive.

To prove they are a qualified entity, the company submits its business plan together with articles of incorporation, financial records, tax records, and stock certificates. To prove the applicant's status as a functional manager, the company submits a detailed job description with specific duties and the names, qualifications, and salaries of the dozens of employees she has managed over time. The application is approved, and this manager, already in the United States on a B-2 visa, changes status to L-1A, and begins work.

L-1 INFOGRAPHICS

The application process involves the filing of an I-129 Petition for a Nonimmigrant Worker with the accompanying L Supplement.

This petition must be submitted to USCIS with the appropriate fee and supporting documentation.

L-1 BENEFICIARIES CURRENTLY IN THE U.S.

If the application is successful,

L-1 beneficiaries can change their status to L-1 without leaving the U.S.

The USCIS issues an I-797 (Notice of Action) which is a notice confirming that the applicant's L petition has been approved.

This form is attached to their departure/entry record (I-94) and their status as an L-1 is affirmed.

APPLICANT IS LIVING OUTSIDE OF THE UNITED STATES

Applicant must make an appointment with an embassy or consulate in their home nation & bring with them their I-797 approval notice.

The consulate/embassy has the power to review & scrutinize supporting documentation to determine the validity of the L-1 petition.

If the application procedure is followed carefully & the supporting documentation is compelling, the L-1 beneficiary will be able to enter the U.S. & begin their work.

During the process there can be additional waiting time because of the appointment requirement. Some embassies/consulates do not have any interview openings for several weeks.

These visas are a valuable tool for **multinational companies and companies wishing to expand their operations in the U.S. or open a U.S. branch or office.**

L-1 INTRACOMPANY TRANSFER VISAS ARE GEARED TOWARD...
Foreign companies wishing to transfer:

- **An executive, manager (L-1A) or**
- **Specialized knowledge employee (L-1B)**
- **to live and work in the U.S. in one of those capacities.**

WHO CAN PETITION FOR AN L-1 EMPLOYEE
An individual cannot apply for L-1 status

The U.S. entity desiring their transfer to the U.S. must petition on their behalf.

This U.S. entity petitioning for the foreign national and the foreign entity where the foreign national has been employed must either be the same company, part of the same company or be related (parent, branch, affiliate or subsidiary).

OTHER REQUIREMENTS
The L-1 visa beneficiary must be transferred to the U.S. to provide the same or similar executive, managerial or specialized knowledge services that he or she provided the foreign entity.

The U.S. organization must be currently conducting business as an employer in both the U.S. & one other country for the duration of the visa beneficiary's stay in the U.S.

The foreign national must have been employed by the qualifying foreign entity for at least one continuous year within the three years prior to entering the U.S. Their employment must have been in an executive, managerial or specialized knowledge capacity as well.

EXECUTIVE, MANAGER & SPECIALIZED KNOWLEDGE WORKER

L-1A Executive – an L-1A qualifying executive must make important decisions without much oversight; he/she must direct the management of the company.

L-1A Manager – an L-1A qualifying manager will have to prove that their management is essential to the proper functioning of the company.

L-1B Specialized Knowledge Employee – the foreign national must be able to prove an advanced understanding of the company, including its processes and if applicable, its products. A specialized knowledge employee must be able to transfer that knowledge abroad, and therefore have an understanding of global markets.

PATH TO
**PERMANENT
RESIDENCE**

FOR THE L-1A EXECUTIVE OR MANAGER WHO DECIDES TO STAY IN THE U.S.

 The best course of action is to apply for an employment based green card & the best option is the EB-1C or Priority Workers: Multinational Executives and Managers visa.

 This visa allows the L-1A applicants to skip the PERM Labor Certification program.

 The beneficiary's employer must petition USCIS, with a Form I-140 (Immigrant Petition for Alien Worker) along with Form I-485 (Application to Register Permanent Residence or Adjust Status).

FOR THE L-1B VISA HOLDER

 PERM Labor Certification Program.

 The path to permanent residence may take longer, but it is possible.

 If the application is ultimately successful an I-140 petition as well as an I-485 petition can be filed and the L-1B (as well as his or her family) can receive green cards and stay in the U.S. permanently.

L-1 FAQS

Q: What are the benefits of applying for an L-1 visa?

A: L-1 visas offer organizations, both large and small, an amazing and unique opportunity, and are mutually beneficial to all parties involved. By facilitating the transfer of executives, managers, and employees with specialized knowledge from a foreign entity to a U.S. office, businesses both abroad and in the United States are able to expand and grow. L-1 visas enable the smaller foreign companies to open a new branch in the United States, thereby reaching new and different market groups previously unattainable or, at the very least, difficult to penetrate.

Larger organizations also take advantage of the opportunities L-1 visas provide to further business development within the United States, as well as to enhance international competitiveness through the melding of novel (perhaps even foreign) concepts brought in by a fresh set of eyes and ears. L-1 visas also offer the beneficiaries and employees an expedited and less expensive route than other employment-based immigrant options.

If permanent residency is not required for the employee, then a green card is unnecessary and may prove to be a waste of time and money. An L-1 visa is a great place to start—the beneficiary can reside and work in the United States for an extended period of time with his/her family for the entirety of the visa's duration, and, should it become necessary for the L-1 visa holder to remain in the United States permanently, it is an easy and painless transition. Additionally, unlike most immigrant visas, there are no annual quotas placed on L-1 visas, and, because L-1 visas are considered dual-intent visas (unlike many other non-immigrant visas), the beneficiary's L-1 status will not be negatively affected should the holder decide to apply for permanent residency.

Q: What is the difference between an L-1A and an L-1B visa?

A: Both visas enable the transfer of a foreign employee to the United States from a foreign office on the condition that they intend to either work in a branch of a qualified entity (parent company, sister organization, branch office, or subsidiary) in the United States, or open a new U.S. office. The major difference between an L-1A and L-1B visa is that an L-1A visa is exclusively intended for the transfer of employees in an executive or managerial capacity, while an L-1B visa is specifically for the transfer of an employee with specialized knowledge, critical to the operations of the U.S. entity.

Q: How do I know if I qualify for an L-1 visa?

A: Unlike an E-2 visa, anyone from any country qualifies as long as they are employed by a qualifying foreign entity for at least one of the previous three years prior to application filing in an executive, managerial, or specialized knowledge capacity. Qualified employees must come to the United States with the intention of working for a (or establishing a new) qualifying U.S. office in a similar capacity as executive, manager, or employee with specialized knowledge.

Q: Are there stay restrictions on the L-1 visa?

A: Yes. L-1A visa beneficiaries can stay in the United States for a maximum of seven years, while holders of an L-1B visa are allowed to stay for a maximum of five years. Beneficiaries must continue to renew L-1 visas every year or two (this varies depending on the conditions of the visa) in order to stay for the maximum allowed period of stay.

Q: Can I bring my spouse and/or children?

A: Yes. Once granted, the spouse and minor children (under age 21) of L-1 visa holders are eligible to apply for an L-2 dependent visa, which is valid for the entire duration of the stay of the L-1 visa holder. Additionally, spouses of L-1 visa aliens may work in the United States on an "as-needed" basis, as long as they apply correctly through USCIS.

Q: How much will my L-1 visa application cost?

A: At the time of this writing, the usual range for the legal and business plan components of the process is $14,000 to $20,000 depending on the complexity and nature of the business and visa qualifications. This does not include the filing fees required by USCIS, which is $825 for the first filing (and $460 for each subsequent visa extension), plus an additional (but not required) $1,225 premium process fee, if you decide to expedite the process. $500 fraud prevention and detection fee must also be included.

Q: If I decide to become a U.S. citizen, is there a direct path toward permanent residence?

A: Yes. If an L-1A holder decided to make his/her stay in the United States a permanent one, he/she can then apply for an employment-based green card, such as EB-1, EB-2, or EB-3. The best option for L-1A beneficiaries is the EB-1C or Priority Workers: Multinational Executives and Managers visa, which, not only has very similar requirements to the L-1A visa application process, but allows L-1A applicants to skip the PERM program (a time-consuming and expensive process used to determine whether or not there are enough qualified U.S. workers available for the job position the alien is seeking) that is required for all other employment-based green card applicants before they begin the application process. Unfortunately, there is no direct path toward permanent residence for an L-1B visa holder, but beneficiaries can still make the transition from non-immigrant to immigrant status through any of the employment-based green card visa options.

Q: What is required for an L-1 visa application?

A: First, there must be a qualifying relationship between the U.S. and foreign entities (parent company, sister organization, branch office, or subsidiary); second, the U.S. organization must currently or will soon be conducting business as an employer in both the United States and one other country for the duration of the visa beneficiary's stay in the United States; third, the alien must have been working for a qualifying foreign entity in a managerial, executive, or specialized knowledge capacity for at least one continuous year within the three consecutive years prior to entering the United States; and, fourth, the employee must intend to provide the qualified U.S. entity with similar executive, managerial, or specialized knowledge services as he/she provided the foreign entity.

Q: What professionals do I need to hire for a successful application?

A: An experienced immigration attorney is a must, as is a qualified business plan provider with experience writing plans that correspond to USCIS's requirements. A single-point-of-contact team to "quarterback" the entire application process is also highly recommended. This "quarterback" will oversee all project components, ensuring a pain-free, cost-effective, and efficient experience.

Q: Can I renew my L-1 visa?

A: Yes. As long as the conditions continue to be met, the visa can be renewed for a maximum stay of seven years for L-1A visa holders and a maximum stay of five years for L-1B visa holders.

Q: How long is my L-1 visa good for?

A: Qualified employees entering the United States with the intention of establishing a new office are allowed to reside in the United States for a maximum initial stay of one year on an L-1A visa. If the alien wants or needs to stay longer, then he/she may request extensions in increments of up to two additional years, and can continue to do so in order to remain in the United States for a total of seven consecutive years.

All other qualified L-1A employees are granted an initial stay of up to three years, and also have the ability to request up to two-year extensions, until he/she has reached a total of seven consecutive years residing in the United States.

Qualified foreign employees intent on establishing a new office will be granted an initial stay of one year on an L-1B visa, with the ability to request extensions for a maximum of two-year increments, until he/she has spent a total of five consecutive years residing and working in the United States. All other qualified L-1B employees will be given a maximum initial stay of up to three years, with the ability to request additional two-year extensions, for a maximum stay of seven consecutive years.

Q: Where/how do I apply for my L-1 visa?

A: The petition must be submitted to USCIS by the U.S. entity (or foreign entity, if establishing a new office). For the application to be successful, petitioners must collect and provide the following documentation to USCIS:

1. A completed Form I-129 (Petition for a Non-immigrant Worker), along with the L Supplement (visit https://www.uscis.gov/i-129);

2. A letter from the U.S. employer confirming that the beneficiary will be employed by them in a qualified capacity in the United States;

3. Documentation evidencing a qualifying relationship between the U.S. and foreign business entities, such as a statement by an authorized official describing relationship of ownership and control between the companies;

4. Documentation that shows the parent company and its subsidiaries, such as Security and Exchange Commission (SEC) filings;

5. Additional evidence of ownership, such as tax returns and records of stock ownership;

6. Financial viability, if the beneficiary is entering the United States to establish a new office or branch;

7. A letter signed by an authorized official detailing the employee's qualifications to work in the United States in a managerial, executive, or specialized knowledge capacity. This includes the job duties, level of authority, as well as salary and dates of employment with the foreign entity; and

8. The required fees.

Q: How long is the L-1 visa application process?

A: Once all the required documentation has been turned in to USCIS, the application process time averages roughly three to five months. But, for an additional fee of $1,225, the petitioning employer can expedite the process through premium processing. By submitting Form 1-907, in conjunction with Form I-129 and the added fee, the petitioner is provided with the premium processing service, which guarantees a fifteen-day turnaround. In other words, within fifteen days of submitting the application, the petitioner will receive an approval notice, denial notice, or a Request for Evidence (RFE).

Q: Are there any travel restrictions on an L-1 visa?

A: No. As long as the visa has not expired, the holder can travel abroad and return to the United States as often as he/she desires.

CHAPTER 3

Introduction to the E Visa Category— Treaty Traders & Investors

"Talented and ambitious immigrants make the U.S. economy great."

—WARREN BUFFETT

The United States maintains treaties of trade and/ or investment with a number of countries as a way of promoting cooperation, stronger binational relationships, commerce, and navigation. These treaties are clearly meant to encourage friendly relations between the nations that are parties to them, but they are also a way of promoting foreign trade and investment, while protecting those same investments in accordance with applicable domestic and international laws.

The United States has entered into treaties since the Revolutionary War, when it sought to get a foothold in trade as an independent nation. After World War I, the United States was acknowledged as a world power and an increased number of treaties were signed, which was further augmented following World War II, when international trade and investment expanded substantially on a global basis.

The continued encouragement of foreign trade and investment, as well as the interest in protecting these investments, gave rise to the E visa program that set guidelines for who, how, when, and for how long foreign nationals would be allowed to enter, live, and work in the United States based on commerce and investment.

Some of these treaties have been in existence for centuries, and some have been added within the last two decades. For example, the United Kingdom and the United States have been parties to a bilateral treaty of trade and commerce since 1815, and Costa Rica and Colombia have been parties to similar treaties since the mid-nineteenth century. On the other hand, the author's home country and the United States' friendliest neighbor to the north, Canada, was not a party to such a bilateral treaty with the United States until 1993, followed closely by the ratification of NAFTA (North American Free Trade Agreement) in 1994, which further opened the borders between Canada and the United States and also added Mexico to the treaty mix (although NAFTA is the subject of current debate under the Trump administration, as are many other free and open trade agreements). For a complete alphabetical list (with links to the complete texts) of all the trade treaties between the United States and the other nations of the world, visit Export.gov (http://tcc.export.gov/Trade_Agreements/All_Trade_Agreements/).

After World War II, the United States sought to facilitate private international investment by signing a Treaty of Friendship, Commerce and Navigation with many more countries than had previously been the case. Since the 1980s, investment provisions were typically included in various Free Trade Agreements (some of which are, as noted, in varied stages of review under the Trump administration) or in standalone compacts called Bilateral Investment Treaties (BITs).

BITs establish the terms and conditions for private investments made by individuals and business entities from one sovereign state in another sovereign state. Typically, nationals from countries that have signed a BIT with the United States are eligible to apply for an E-1 or E-2 visa. (Note: the E-1 Treaty Trader visa is much less coveted or utilized than the E-2 Treaty Investor visa, as will be discussed further in Chapters 4 and 5).

BITs are based on the concept of reciprocity. As such, they obligate foreign countries to provide American investors and companies with the same protections and rights that their citizens would receive in the United States. BITs further require that investors and their investments be treated "as favorably as the host party treats its own investors and their investments or investors and investments from any third country."

In addition to granting investors from a contracting state "fair and equitable treatment," BITs also provide for the free transfer of funds in and out of the country as well as protection from expropriation. If an expropriation does happen, BITs ensure that investors are compensated in a fair and timely manner. BITs also provide investors recourse to arbitration, often under the auspices of the International Centre for Settlement of Investment Disputes (ICSID), to resolve disputes with the host state. In sum, contracting countries must treat private investments in an open, transparent, predictable, and nondiscriminatory manner.

The United States lacks confidence in the ability of many countries to guarantee the aforementioned protections and rights to *American investors* if Americans were seeking to invest *into* said countries, such that these countries remain ineligible to enter into a BIT with the United States. Countries that are subject to international sanction or with which the United States has poor relations may also be excluded from such opportunities. However, there are many other reasons for the lack of a BIT—sometimes it is due to a lack of perceived *need,* while other times it might be politically driven, as the author would purport has been the case with Israel.[1]

The explanation as to why a particular country has not yet concluded a BIT with the United States is often complex, case-specific, highly politicized, and not always made public by the U.S. government. Noticeably absent are all of the BRICS countries—Brazil, Russia, India, China, and South Africa. These emerging economies do not currently have treaties of commerce and navigation with the United States, so aliens from those countries must find alternatives to work in the United States, such as

---

1. In 2012, President Obama signed legislation adding Israel to the list of eligible E-2 visa treaty nations, thereby presumably opening the U.S. markets to Israeli investors seeking entrée to the United States; however, for a variety of reasons, Israel has been slow to implement the Israeli version of the E-2, known as the B-5 visa. Hopefully, by the time this book is published, this will have been resolved and the E-2 with Israel will have been fully implemented and ratified—most stakeholders both within Israel and/or abroad but working with many Israelis are confident that this will occur by 3rd quarter 2017. NOTE: Israel has been an E-1 Treaty Trader country since 1954!

L-1 visas or EB-5 visas,[2] which do not restrict by nation or nationality. In some cases, citizens of BRICS countries or other nations that do not have appropriate treaties in place with the United States may hold or be eligible to apply for other passports, which may enable them to access an E visa category. Additionally, nationals from countries that do not have an investor treaty with the United States sometimes seek to invest in countries that in turn allow them to qualify for citizenship by investment, such as Grenada or Cyprus, which in turn allows them to apply for an E visa.

If the alien applicant is a citizen of one of the nations with which the United States has a treaty of friendship, commerce, and navigation, or the equivalent, he/she is eligible for E-1 and/or E-2 classification. These visa classifications are *only* available to foreign nationals from treaty countries.

There are many commonalities between the two visa categories, as outlined further below. For example, there is no dual intent permitted for E-1 or E-2 visa holders, as will be outlined further in Chapters 4 and 5, an applicant must specifically note his/her intent to return to his/her home country at the expiration of the applicable visa and/or if the subject business ceases operations.

It is important to note that the length of the time granted by an E visa varies based on the alien's country

---

2. Until 2015, applicants born in mainland China used approximately 85 percent of the available EB-5 visas (total of 10,000 per year). Travel.state.gov (https://travel.state.gov/content/visas/en/law-and-policy/statistics/annual-reports/report-of-the-visa-office-2015.html) notes that in 2015 Chinese applicants accounted for 7,616 of the total 8,773 EB-5 visa numbers issued.

of nationality and the applicable reciprocity schedule (visit https://travel.state.gov/content/visas/en/fees/reciprocity-by-country.html). The maximum time for the *visa* is usually five years, which will usually also apply to the spouse and children. However, although the duration of the visa itself might be five years, most E visa holders are usually granted two-year periods of stay. E visa holders can then apply for extensions of stay in increments of not more than two years. To qualify, the treaty trader/investor must be in valid E-status, and must file an application for extension of stay using Form I-129 and an E-Supplement, together with the required supplementary documents.

Alternatively, the visa holder can depart the United States and seek reentry with the valid visa for an additional two years; there is no limit to the number of times this can be done. In both cases, to qualify for an extension, the alien must prove that he/she: 1) has at all times maintained the terms and conditions of his/her E non-immigrant classification, 2) was physically present in the United States at the time of filing the application for extension of stay, and 3) has not abandoned his/her extension request. The alien can also depart and reenter the United States freely during the term of the visa, and at the time of reentry will usually be granted an additional year. Additionally, USCIS must approve any substantive change in the terms or conditions of E-1 or E-2 status.[3]

There is also a unique classification available to E-1 or E-2 employees, the qualifications of which are that the employee must:

- Be the same nationality as the principal alien employer (who must have the nationality of the treaty country);

- Meet the definition of "employee" under the relevant law; and

- Either be engaging in duties of an executive or *supervisory character,* or if employed in a lesser capacity, have special qualifications (the latter of which means that the services are essential to the business's efficient operations).[4]

There are many cases wherein the alien employer is a company, in which case it must be at least 50 percent owned by people in the United States who possess the relevant treaty country's nationality and maintain treaty trader (E-1) or treaty investor (E-2) status.[5]

---

3. A "substantive change" is defined as a fundamental change in the employer's basic characteristics, such as, but not limited to, a merger, acquisition, or major event that affects the treaty investor or employee's previously approved relationship with the organization. The treaty investor or enterprise must notify USCIS by filing a new Form I-129 with fee, and may simultaneously request an extension of stay for the treaty investor or affected employee. The Form I-129 must include evidence to show that the treaty investor or affected employee continues to qualify for E-2 classification. (Source: uscis.gov)

4. U.S. Citizenship and Immigration Services. "Temporary (Nonimmigrant) Workers." USCIS. Accessed April 25, 2017. www.uscis.gov/working-united-states/temporary-nonimmigrant-workers.

5. Employee of Treaty Trader and Treaty Investor, 8 CFR 214.2(e)(3)(ii). UCCIS.gov. Accessed April 25,2017. https://www.uscis.gov/ilink/docView/FR/HTML/FR/0-0-0-1/0-0-0-30133/0-0-0-39631/0-0-0-41149/0-0-0-41197.html.

Families of E-1/E-2 Visa Beneficiaries

One of the benefits of applying for an E-1 or E-2 visa is that upon arrival in the United States, the visa beneficiary's spouse can apply for a social security number and work authorization and his/her children (under age 21) can attend school in the United States for the duration of the visa term, although the children are not granted work authorization.

The Path to Permanent Residence

Since both E-1 and E-2 visas are non-immigrant in both nature and intent, there is no *direct* path to permanent residence available by way of either E classification. However, there are a few *indirect* routes that enable E visa holders to pursue the path to permanent residence.

Permanent residence is really *not necessary* in the case of E-1 or E-2 visas provided that the visa holder can prove that he/she is continuing to engage in ongoing treaty trader/investor activities, as outlined above. The holder can also depart and re-enter the United States freely with a consular-issued E visa. However, for many E visa holders, going through the renewal process every two to five years can become cumbersome, and as time goes by, this visa holder may become desirous to live and work permanently in the United States, thus seeking an alternate path to permanent residence.

One way of achieving this is to change status to that of an EB-5 investor, which is a much more common path for E-2 treaty investors than for E-1 treaty traders, in large part because the original E-2 investment capital can be used as the basis for the generally larger EB-5 minimum investment threshold (see further discussion herein). Because of its complexity, EB-5 status will be discussed in detail beginning in Chapter 8, but generally speaking, it involves an investment of $1,000,000 or $500,000 (depending upon the location) as of the date of this writing and the creation of at least ten jobs for U.S. workers. For both E-1 and E-2 visa holders, this would require significant additional investment in the United States, which investment must be sourced from the visa holder's personal assets (i.e., the additional investment cannot be from reinvested business income, but rather must be invested directly from the applicant's personal funds or must be drawn from the business and allocated directly to the investor's personal funds in order to "count"). EB-5 approval translates to conditional permanent residence (initially) for the investor and his/ her family, which conditions can be removed upon the submission and approval of the appropriate petition not less than two years after the granting of the conditional permanent resident status.

Another route is for either the visa holder or his/ her spouse to secure a job with a company willing to sponsor an H-1B visa and following that path to permanent residence. This, of course, would mean giving up entrepreneurship, but for some applicants, owning and operating a business could prove to be too taxing and going the corporate route becomes an option if permanent residence is the ultimate goal. Additionally, if the E-1 or E-2 visa holder's spouse finds work as an H-1B, that spouse can follow the path to permanent residence, taking his/her spouse along for the ride.

E-1/E-2 VISA FACTS INFOGRAPHICS

Applying for an E-Visa While in the United States

If the applicant is present under a temporary business visa (B-1), he/she can change his/her status to E-visa by filing a Form I-129 (Petition for a Nonimmigrant Worker) with USCIS. The applicant must pay the applicable filing fee and provide all required documentation. The applicant will need to include a statement, (usually a written statement is enough), of their intent to return to their home country after the expiration of their E-1/E-2 visa and the conclusion of their business dealings since this visa is also temporary in intent (although renewals are also available).

Applying for an E-Visa at a U.S. Embassy or Consulate

Applying while outside of the United States requires applying online to the U.S. Department of State using a form DS-160, payment of filing fee and provision of all required documentation. An appointment with the appropriate Embassy or Consulate will need to be scheduled, and waiting times will vary.

Applying for an E-Visa While in the United States

The foreign national can apply to change his/her status to E-1 or E-2 by filing a Form I-129 (Petition for a Nonimmigrant Worker) with USCIS and paying the filing fee. If the applicant satisfies the requirements and provides the requested documentation, (s)he will be granted E-status for a two-year period. The applicant will need to include a statement (usually a written statement is enough) of their intent to return to their home country after the expiration of their E-1 visa and the conclusion of their business dealings since this visa is also temporary in intent (although renewals are also available).

TABLE 3.1. E-1/E-2 TREATY COUNTRIES WITH DATES

COUNTRY	CLASSIFICATION	EFFECTIVE DATE
Albania	E-2	January 4, 1998
Argentina	E-1	October 20, 1994
Argentina	E-2	October 20, 1994
Armenia	E-2	March 29, 1996
Australia	E-1	December 16, 1991
Australia	E-2	December 27, 1991
Austria	E-1	May 27, 1931
Austria	E-2	May 27, 1931
Azerbaijan	E-2	August 2, 2001
Bahrain	E-2	May 30, 2001
Bangladesh	E-2	July 25, 1989
Belgium	E-1	October 3, 1963
Belgium	E-2	October 3, 1963
Bolivia	E-1	November 09, 1862
Bolivia	E-2	June 6, 2001
Bosnia and Herzegovina	E-1	November 15, 1882
Bosnia and Herzegovina	E-2	November 15, 1882
Brunei	E-1	July 11, 1853
Bulgaria	E-2	June 2, 1994
Cameroon	E-2	April 6, 1989
Canada	E-1	January 1, 1993

Canada	E-2	January 1, 1993
Chile	E-1	January 1, 2004
Chile	E-2	January 1, 2004
China (Taiwan)	E-1	November 30, 1948
China (Taiwan)	E-2	November 30, 1948
Colombia	E-1	June 10, 1848
Colombia	E-2	June 10, 1848
Congo (Brazzaville)	E-2	August 13, 1994
Congo (Kinshasa)	E-2	July 28, 1989
Costa Rica	E-1	May 26, 1852
Costa Rica	E-2	May 26, 1852
Croatia	E-1	November 15, 1882
Croatia	E-2	November 15, 1882
Czech Republic	E-2	January 1, 1993
Denmark	E-1	July 30, 1961
Denmark	E-2	December 10, 2008
Ecuador	E-2	May 11, 1997
Egypt	E-2	June 27, 1992
Estonia	E-1	May 22, 1926
Estonia	E-2	February 16, 1997
Ethiopia	E-1	October 8, 1953
Ethiopia	E-2	October 8, 1953
Finland	E-1	August 10, 1934
Finland	E-2	December 1, 1992

France	E-1	December 21, 1960
France	E-2	December 21, 1960
Georgia	E-2	August 17, 1997
Germany	E-1	July 14, 1956
Germany	E-2	July 14, 1956
Greece	E-1	October 13, 1954
Grenada	E-2	March 3, 1989
Honduras	E-1	July 19, 1928
Honduras	E-2	July 19, 1928
Iran	E-1	June 16, 1957
Iran	E-2	June 16, 1957
Ireland	E-1	September 14, 1950
Ireland	E-2	November 18, 1992
Israel	E-1	April 3, 1954
Italy	E-1	July 26, 1949
Italy	E-2	July 26, 1949
Jamaica	E-2	March 7, 1997
Japan	E-1	October 30, 1953
Japan	E-2	October 30, 1953
Jordan	E-1	December 17, 2001
Jordan	E-2	December 17, 2001
Kazakhstan	E-2	January 12, 1994
Korea (South)	E-1	November 7, 1957
Korea (South)	E-2	November 7, 1957

Kosovo	E-1	November 15, 1882
Kosovo	E-2	November 15, 1882
Kyrgyzstan	E-2	January 12, 1994
Latvia	E-1	July 25, 1928
Latvia	E-2	December 26, 1996
Liberia	E-1	November 21, 1939
Liberia	E-2	November 21, 1939
Lithuania	E-2	November 22, 2001
Luxembourg	E-1	March 28, 1963
Luxembourg	E-2	March 28, 1963
Macedonia	E-1	November 15, 1882
Macedonia	E-2	November 15, 1882
Mexico	E-1	January 1, 1994
Mexico	E-2	January 1, 1994
Moldova	E-2	November 25, 1994
Mongolia	E-2	January 1, 1997
Montenegro	E-1	November 15, 1882
Montenegro	E-2	November 15, 1882
Morocco	E-2	May 29, 1991
Netherlands	E-1	December 5, 1957
Netherlands	E-2	December 5, 1957
Norway	E-1	January 18, 1928
Norway	E-2	January 18, 1928
Oman	E-1	June 11, 1960

Oman	E-2	June 11, 1960
Pakistan	E-1	February 12, 1961
Pakistan	E-2	February 12, 1961
Panama	E-2	May 30, 1991
Paraguay	E-1	March 07, 1860
Paraguay	E-2	March 07, 1860
Philippines	E-1	September 6, 1955
Philippines	E-2	September 6, 1955
Poland	E-1	August 6, 1994
Poland	E-2	August 6, 1994
Romania	E-2	January 15, 1994
Serbia	E-1	November 15,1882
Serbia	E-2	November 15,1882
Senegal	E-2	October 25, 1990
Singapore	E-1	January 1, 2004
Singapore	E-2	January 1, 2004
Slovak Republic	E-2	January 1, 1993
Slovenia	E-1	November 15, 1882
Slovenia	E-2	November 15, 1882
Spain	E-1	April 14, 1903
Spain	E-2	April 14, 1903
Sri Lanka	E-2	May 1, 1993
Suriname	E-1	February 10, 1963
Suriname	E-2	February 10, 1963

Sweden	E-1	February 20, 1992
Sweden	E-2	February 20, 1992
Switzerland	E-1	November 08, 1855
Switzerland	E-2	November 08, 1855
Thailand	E-1	June 8, 1968
Thailand	E-2	June 8, 1968
Togo	E-1	February 5, 1967
Togo	E-2	February 5, 1967
Trinidad & Tobago	E-2	December 26, 1996
Tunisia	E-2	February 7, 1993
Turkey	E-1	February 15, 1933
Turkey	E-2	May 18, 1990
Ukraine	E-2	November 16, 1996
United Kingdom	E-1	July 03, 1815
United Kingdom	E-2	July 03, 1815
Yugoslavia	E-1	November 15, 1882
Yugoslavia	E-2	November 15, 1882

Source: https://travel.state.gov/content/visas/en/fees/treaty.html

CHAPTER 4

E-1 Non-immigrant Visas (Treaty Trader)— The Forgotten Visa

"I received a letter just before I left office from a man. I don't know why he chose to write it, but I'm glad he did. He wrote that you can go to live in France, but you can't become a Frenchman. You can go to live in Germany or Italy, but you can't become a German, an Italian. He went through Turkey, Greece, Japan and other countries. But he said anyone, from any corner of the world, can come to live in the United States..."

—RONALD REAGAN, 40TH PRESIDENT OF THE UNITED STATES

As noted in Chapter 3, in an effort to encourage the global economy and inspire friendly relations and trade between nations, the E visa category was developed. It has given entrepreneurs a pathway to live and work in the United States, but not a direct pathway to permanent residence. It remains a non-immigrant visa classification with a built-in "intent to return" requirement. However, it is a renewable visa with potentially unlimited renewals, provided the applicant satisfies the criteria.

The E-1 (Treaty Trader) non-immigrant visa is a good choice for foreign nationals who are interested in engaging in trade between the United States and the trader's home country (again, the home country must be a treaty trader nation). Unlike its counterpart, the E-2 (Treaty Investor) visa, an E-1 visa does not require a substantial capital investment but merely proof that there exists substantial business (or the trading of goods and services for profit) between the applicant and the United States. Table 4.1 on the following page highlights the number of E-1 visas granted between 2013 and 2015 to each respective nation.

Requirements of an E-1 Visa

The E-1 visa applicant will be granted this classification if he/she can prove to the satisfaction of the adjudicator that they engage in substantial trade with the United States and plan to continue and/or expand that trade by living and working on American soil. The applicant can do business on his/her own behalf and can apply for an E-1 visa for him/herself and for a certain number of employees if those employees are vital to the success of the business because of expertise or education.

It is critical to understand clearly what "trade" means. "Trade" is defined by the U.S. immigration service as the existing international exchange of goods or services that have an extrinsic value and are traded for profit. When we think of trade, we often think of the import/export of goods such as automobiles, furniture, textiles, gems, precious metals, or electronic equipment. These are all

TABLE 4.1. E-1 VISA STATISTICS BY TREATY NATION*		
TREATY NATION	**YEAR**	**NUMBER OF E-1 VISAS ISSUED**
Argentina	2013; 2014; 2015	33; 67; 45
Australia	2013; 2014; 2015	40; 21; 33
Belgium	2013; 2014; 2015	6; 20; 19
Canada	2013; 2014; 2015	363; 446; 450
Colombia	2013; 2014; 2015	4; 84; 73
France	2013; 2014; 2015	172; 139; 155
Germany	2013; 2014; 2015	1,317; 1,449; 1,426
Israel	2013; 2014; 2015	340; 225; 377
Italy	2013; 2014; 2015	245; 306; 325
Japan	2013; 2014; 2015	1,625; 1,799; 1,724
Mexico	2013; 2014; 2015	1,198; 1,154; 1,139
Poland	2013; 2014; 2015	3; 4; 12
Spain	2013; 2014; 2015	112; 100; 89
Thailand	2013; 2014; 2015	28; 30; 24
Turkey	2013; 2014; 2015	33; 57; 55
United Kingdom	2013; 2014; 2015	219; 155; 204
Venezuela	2013; 2014; 2015	1; 0; 1

Data provided by the U.S. Department of State; not all treaty nations are included.

businesses that an E-1 applicant could be involved in and continue while living and working in the United States.

In addition, USCIS also recognizes business enterprises in the fields of international banking, tourism, insurance, and communications as E-1 eligible enterprises. These enterprises do not trade in tangible goods but instead provide services for profit that are more difficult to value, but are eligible nonetheless. The immigration service requires that whatever the nature of the trade, whether it is goods or services, the trading activity must be clearly defined and described on the visa application.

A specific number or monetary value doesn't define the substantial trade requirement, but the higher the monetary value of the goods or services, the stronger the application. Even more important than the monetary value is the frequency of trade. *Substantial* may not have a value attached, but *frequency* is understood in the definition. The alien applicant must engage in enough trade to show a viable business yielding a net profit that can support him/her and a potential spouse and children.

In addition to the qualification of substantial trade, for the E-1 visa classification to be successful, the applicant must prove that he/she carries on *principal* trade between the United States and the home country (a treaty nation). USCIS defines "principal trade" as more than 50 percent of the applicant's total volume of international trade. In a corporate scenario or with a business that is owned in a fifty-fifty partnership, at least one of the partners must be from a treaty nation.

Applying for an E-1 Visa While in the United States

If a foreign national is already in the United States with another lawful non-immigrant status, for instance, if he/she is present under a temporary business visa (B-1), he/she can change his/her status to E-1 by filing a Form I-129 (Petition for a Non-immigrant Worker) with USCIS. The filing fee for this application is $460 at the time of this writing, but fees change periodically so it is best to visit the USCIS website (https://www.uscis.gov/sites/default/files/files/form/g-1055.pdf) for an updated list of filing fees.

If the applicant meets the requirements outlined and provides the requested documentation, he/she will be granted E-1 status for two years. The applicant must also include a statement (usually a written statement is sufficient) of his/her intent to return to the home country after the expiration of his/her E-1 visa and the conclusion of the U.S. business dealings.

The downside of applying directly with USCIS for a change of status to E-1 is that E visas fall under the jurisdiction of the U.S. Department of State. Therefore, when filing a change of status with USCIS, a change of status is all that is being granted, not a visa. The E-1 visa is issued by the U.S. Department of State, and if the applicant needs to travel outside of the United States for any reason, he/she will have to reapply at a U.S. consular post to regain entry into the United States with that visa to continue trading. For that reason, many applicants choose to apply for an E visa in their home country at the outset and enter into the United States having already been granted an E-1 visa.[1]

Those who choose to change their status with USCIS may believe they won't have to travel home in the next two years or don't want to interrupt their busy lives to go home, apply for an E-1 visa, gather the documentation, wait for an appointment, wait for processing, and run the risk of a failed petition, but applying for an E-1 visa through an embassy or consular post does come with fewer restrictions.

Applying for an E-1 Visa at a U.S. Embassy or Consulate

Applying for an E-1 treaty trader visa while outside of the United States requires the submission of an online application to the U.S. Department of State using Form DS-160. The fee associated with this application is $205 at the time of this writing, but these fees change periodically. It is best to visit the U.S. Department of State website for up-to-date filing fees (https://travel.state.gov/content/visas/en/employment/treaty.html). A list of U.S. embassies and consulates can be found at www.usembassy.gov, and respective individual websites will detail the procedure for applying for an E-1 treaty trader visa.

---

1. USCIS recently introduced a new web-based program called VIBE (VIBE = Validation Instrument for Business Enterprises). VIBE was designed to improve USCIS's adjudications of certain employment-based immigration visas using commercially available data from such sources as Dun & Bradstreet to validate basic information about petitioning organizations seeking to employ foreign nationals.

One upside of applying for an E-1 visa at an embassy or consulate is that, if approved, the treaty trader is granted entry for two years and can come and go as he/she pleases once in the United States. Every two years, the E-1 visa is renewable indefinitely as long as frequent and substantial trade continues.

The E-1 treaty trader non-immigrant visa is an excellent choice for the businessperson seeking to expand trade between their home nation and the United States but who perhaps lacks enough capital to make a qualifying monetary investment to start or purchase a business in the United States, as required for the E-2 and EB-5; alternatively, the E-1 visa might be selected as it may be the only viable option for foreign nationals from countries that do not have access to the E-2 visa, such as Israel (as of this writing). The E-1 visa offers flexibility, continuity, and potential for unlimited renewals, making it appealing to a large cross section of treaty nation applicants.

REAL-LIFE E-1 SCENARIOS

Scenario 1

Mr. X has owned a successful business in London selling antiques and recently specializing in American Revolutionary War collectibles. As this area of his business has grown, he finds himself frequently traveling to New York and Boston in search of items to purchase and sell in his London store.

Over the last few years, Mr. X has developed relationships with several antique dealers in the United States and is importing close to $250,000 worth of goods from American dealers. He has decided to take his trading to the next level by living in the United States for a period of time and solidifying his contacts as well as establishing new ones and finding the best collectibles for his clients in the UK.

He has adjusted the inventory in his London store to the point where 60 percent of the items he has for sale are American Revolutionary War collectibles. He is able to return to London with a few verbal and written contracts from American dealers that will ensure he has a steady stream of import/export items to fulfill the qualifications of substantial and principal trade. He begins the process of filling out the necessary forms to renter the United States with an E-1 treaty trader visa for a two-year period.

Scenario 2

Mrs. Y has been an educator for decades in her native Copenhagen and prides herself on being a master of several different languages, including English. She has developed a proprietary language learning system that she knows will be a huge success in the United States because it makes learning new languages fun and focuses on the practical. She has had great success throughout Scandinavia and is ready to grow an exchange program with the United States. She would like to sell her method to language schools in the United States, along with establishing an exchange program that allows students to spend four weeks in Copenhagen, Stockholm, Oslo, and Helsinki, and brings Scandinavian students to the

United States to study and promote global communication and international relations.

Mrs. Y enters the United States on a B-1 business visa in the hopes that she can secure some contracts and begin making this trade dream a reality. Her trip to the United States is successful and several large language schools are interested in utilizing not only her language learning system, but also promote the exchange program. She returns to Copenhagen to finalize plans and begin her ultimately successful application for an E-1 treaty trader visa.

E-1 DOCUMENTATION CHECKLIST

APPLICATION FORM

a) **DS-160** Visa Application form for each applicant, with photograph and application fee receipt attached.

b) **DS-156 E**, including a Part III form for each principal applicant (i.e., investor or employee), **fully** completed.

c) Photocopy of **biographic information** pages of passport for each applicant.

d) If applicant is in the United States, copy of current I-94 or I-797.

e) Copy of E visa MRV fee receipt.

EVIDENCE OF OWNERSHIP AND NATIONALITY OF BUSINESS

a) Photocopy of data page of business owner's passport (if different from principal applicant).

b) Documentation of percentage of ownership of the business, e.g., share certificates, partnership agreements, stock exchange listing.

EVIDENCE OF TRADE: E-1 APPLICATION ONLY

a) Documentation of trade conducted, e.g., copies of invoices, bills of lading, U.S. customs declarations, accounts receivable/payable ledgers.

b) Copies of most recent U.S. tax return and/or annual financial report.

c) Copies of broker license or other license needed to conduct trade.

ADDITIONAL DOCUMENTATION FOR E-1/E-2 EMPLOYEE VISAS

a) Detailed job description, including job title, responsibilities, supervisory authority.

b) Organizational Chart reflecting the position and clearly delineating lines of authority.

c) Company letter indicating other E-1/E-2 visa holders in the United States and their positions in the company and the number of U.S. nationals in the firm and their positions in the company.

d) Curriculum vitae or resume of the employee.

e) If applying from the United States: current I-94 or I-797 form.

ADDITIONAL DOCUMENTATION FOR DEPENDENTS

a) Copy of marriage certificate.

b) Copy of birth certificate for dependent children.

E-1 INFOGRAPHICS

REQUIREMENTS FOR AN **E-1 VISA**

The E-1 visa applicant will be granted this classification if he/she can prove to the satisfaction of the adjudicator that they engage in substantial trade with their country of origin and plan to continue and/or expand that trade by living and working on American soil.

 Whatever the nature of the trade, whether it is goods or services, the trading activity must be clearly defined and described on the visa application.

 The alien applicant must engage in sufficient trade to demonstrate a viable business yielding a net profit that can support him/her and his/her immediate family.

 The applicant must prove that they conduct principal trade between the U.S. and their home country AND the home country must have in place a Treaty of Trade & Commerce with the U.S.

E-1 NON-IMMIGRANT VISAS
(TREATY TRADER)

 It is suitable for an individual or certain employees of a company, but it is restricted to individuals and companies of treaty nations only.

 It is a pathway to live and work in the United States, but not a direct pathway to permanent residence.

 It is a good choice for foreign nationals who are interested in engaging in trade with the United States and their home country.

 It does not require a substantial capital investment but merely proof that there exists substantial business between the applicant and the United States.

 This visa is an excellent choice for the businessperson seeking to expand trade between their home nation and the U.S. but who *lacks enough capital* to make a qualifying monetary investment to start or purchase a business in the U.S.

 The E-1 visa offers **flexibility, continuity and potential for unlimited renewals** making it appealing to a large cross section of treaty nation applicants.

E-1 FAQS

Q: What is the difference between an E-1 and an E-2 visa?

A: An E-1 visa is a Treaty *Trader* visa, meaning that the beneficiary must prove that his/her business is (or will soon be) engaged in substantial trade between the United States and the qualifying treaty nation (of which they must be a citizen). For an E-1 visa, there must be evidence that substantial trade exists between the United States and entities from the applicant's home nation. On the other hand, an E-2 is a Treaty *Investor* visa and therefore requires a substantial capital investment in a "non-marginal" enterprise. Both E-1 and E-2 visas are temporary and can be renewed indefinitely as long as the conditions continue to be met. Beneficiaries are required to renew their E-1 visa every two years versus up to every five years for an E-2 visa.

Q: What are the benefits of applying for an E-1 visa?

A: It is the best choice for a businessperson from a treaty nation seeking to expand trade between their home nation and the United States. The E-1 visa offers flexibility, continuity, and is cheaper and faster than the green card application process.

Q: How do I know if I qualify for an E-1 visa?

A: If the visa applicant is a citizen of one of the fifty-four eligible treaty countries, he/she qualifies for an E-1 visa. (Visit https://travel.state.gov/content/visas/en/fees/treaty.html for a complete list of all qualifying E-1 and E-2 Treaty Countries.) Additionally, the applicant must prove that he/she is currently engaged in substantial trade with the United States and that he/she intends to expand/continue that trade between the United States and the treaty nation by living and working in the United States. The applicant can either be an individual of the treaty nation or certain qualified company employees (the employees must also be citizens of the treaty nation to qualify) vital to the success of the business.

Q: Must substantial trade exist before I submit my application?

A: Yes. The applicant must be able to prove that substantial trade exists between the United States' business and entities from the foreign national's home country to qualify.

Q: What happens if my business venture fails?

A: The business must become self-sustaining within its first two years of operations. If the business is successful, the holder can apply for an E-1 visa renewal. If the business fails within the first two years, then the visa will become invalid and the holder must leave the United States immediately, even if the visa has not expired yet. In the case of an E-1 visa, it is advisable not to rely solely on one trading partner, but to develop relationships with others to cover possible future changes or developments that may adversely affect E-1 status.

Q: Can I bring my spouse and/or children?

A: Yes. The beneficiary's spouse and/or unmarried children under age twenty-one are eligible to reside in the

United States for the duration of the beneficiary's E-1 visa. Additionally, the E-1 visa's spouse may work while residing in the United States, as long as he/she applies for a work authorization from USCIS. While dependents of the beneficiary may go to school in the United States, only the spouse may work, whereas children are not eligible to work.

Q: What qualifies as substantial trade?

A: Enough trade volume to ensure continuous flow of international trade between the United States and the treaty country qualifies as substantial trade. While USCIS does not specify a minimum volume or value, the business must engage in enough trade to yield a net profit large enough to support him/herself and any dependents. Additionally, more than 50 percent of the applicant's total volume of international trade must be with the foreign national's home country.

Q: How much will my E-1 visa application cost me?

A: If done correctly the first time around (hiring a qualified team of knowledgeable and experienced experts), the applicant is looking at anywhere from $14,000 to $20,000 (depending on the complexity and nature of the business, as well as visa qualifications, which can vary on a country-by-country basis) for the legal and business plan components of the process.

Q: What is required for an E-1 visa application?

A: Proof that trade between the U.S. and the home country makes up more than 50% of the total volume of international trade is required. The applicant needs to engage in enough trade to show a viable business yielding a net profit that can support self and family. At least 50 percent of the company's ownership must be by a national from a qualifying treaty country.

Q: What professionals do I need to hire for a successful application?

A: An experienced immigration attorney is a must, as is a qualified business plan provider with experience writing plans that correspond to USCIS requirements. A single-point-of-contact team to "quarterback" the entire application process is also highly recommended. This "quarterback" will oversee all project components, ensuring a pain-free, cost-effective, and efficient experience. For more information on the importance of a single source quarterback and professional team, see Chapter 12.

Q: Can I renew my E-1 visa?

A: Yes. It is possible to renew an E-1 visa once every two years, but the renewability of an E-1 visa is contingent on the success of the business. The applicant must prove that the business continues to satisfy the conditions of the E-1 visa to remain in the United States. As long as the holder continues to meet the visa requirements, he/she can generally renew the E-1 visa indefinitely.

Q: Where do I apply for my E-1 visa?

A: At the respective consulate of the treaty nation from which the applicant is applying.

Q: *How long is the E-1 application process?*

A: Processing time generally takes three to four weeks, but varies depending on the consulate's workload.

Q: *Are there any travel restrictions on an E-1 visa?*

A: No. You may travel as often as you like prior to your E-1 expiration.

CHAPTER 5

E-2 Non-immigrant Visas (Treaty Investor)— The Coveted Visa

"America is a nation that welcomes all those who share [our] ideals and values. We have always drawn strength from the brightest and most dedicated people coming here and reaching for the American dream."

—BARACK H. OBAMA,
44TH PRESIDENT OF THE UNITED STATES

For a significant percentage of citizens of other nations who come to the United States to live and work ("foreign nationals"), a pivotal component of their American Dream is to own a business. The concept of building something from the ground up or scaling an existing enterprise holds significant appeal for foreign nationals who come from countries where perhaps business ownership opportunities are rare due to rigid class systems, political instability, a weak economy, or other matters.

In addition, whether completely factual or not, the United States has always been viewed as an entrepreneur's paradise. In recent years, statistics don't necessarily put the United States in the lead (when compared to other Western democracies) with regard to business ownership opportunities, startups,[1] or even small business growth, but perception is everything and the world perceives the United States as the gold standard of entrepreneurship.

The United States may not be the world leader, but the innovations and accomplishments of American entrepreneurs are well known and globally acknowledged, and opportunities in the United States remain virtually endless as do prospective immigrants seeking a new home. There is great satisfaction in entrepreneurship, despite its insistence upon self-discipline, unflappable motivation, and tireless effort. For the foreign national who longs to hang out his/her shingle on U.S. soil, the government offers an accessible and attractive work visa option in the form of an E-2 non-immigrant visa.

The E-2 non-immigrant visa seems to be tailor-made for foreign nationals who are interested in starting or taking over a business in the United States. While its counterpart, the E-1 (Treaty Trader) non-immigrant visa, requires a substantial amount of trade between the national of a treaty country and the United States, the E-2 visa requires a substantial investment of capital in a viable business in the United States with significant risk to the applicant.

USCIS defines a substantial investment as:

"Substantial in relationship to the total cost of either purchasing an established enterprise or establishing

---

1. Note that Israel is commonly known as THE STARTUP NATION due to the unmatched number of startups per capita.

a new one; sufficient to ensure the treaty investor's financial commitment to the successful operation of the enterprise; of a magnitude to support the likelihood that the treaty investor will successfully develop and direct the enterprise. The lower the cost of the enterprise, the higher, proportionately, the investment must be to be considered substantial."[2]

The subject business can be a startup or an established business, but the alien applicant must have a considerable amount of "skin in the game" and his/her intent must be to direct or run the business while in the United States. The general consensus is that "substantiality" differs for service versus product businesses, and based on the expenditures involved in starting the business, for example. It has been the author's experience that the average E-2 visa applicant invests capital in the range of $100,000 or more; if the investment amount is below $100,000, the business plan and petition need to be that much stronger to prove the investment amount is appropriate.

This visa can potentially be renewed indefinitely every five years, and there is no limit to the number of E-2 visas that are issued, making it all the more attractive. It must be noted that the actual term of the visa depends on the reciprocity between the United States and each individual treaty nation. For example, an E-2 visa issued to a Polish national can be renewed multiple times, but it

2. U.S. Citizenship and Immigration Services. "E-2 Treaty Investors." USCIS. Accessed April 24, 2017. www.uscis.gov/working-united-states/temporary-workers/e-2-treaty-investors.

is valid for only one year at a time. For a country such as Iran, where trade was suspended in 1995 because of poor diplomatic relations (thereby making Iranians ineligible for an E-1 trader visa), an E-2 visa can be issued but its validity period is significantly lower. Only one entry into the United States is allowed (as opposed to multiple entries for Polish nationals), restricting travel, and the validity period of an E-2 for an Iranian national is only three months.

As discussed, the E-2 is a renewable visa, but specific attention should be paid to the fact that the applicant must continue to satisfy the necessary qualifications of E-2 status every time the visa is renewed.

Eligible Treaty Nations

With regard to the eligible treaty nations, the information provided in the beginning of Chapter 3 applies here as well. Review pages 47–53 once again. For an up-to-date, comprehensive list of treaty nations, visit https://travel.state.gov/content/visas/en/fees/treaty.html. This site reveals not only the treaty country list but also specifies up-to-date whether the applicable country's citizens are eligible for E-1 or E-2 status, or both. In all, seventy-eight countries maintain current E-2 eligible treaties with the United States at the time of this writing.

Requirements of an E-2 Visa

Once it has been established that the alien applicant is a national of a treaty nation, more focus can be placed on determining whether he/she qualifies with regard to his/her proposed investment. Because the purpose of the E-2 visa is to help make a positive impact on the American economy, certain investment requirements must be met before the visa is granted.

This particular visa is document intensive (a document checklist is included on page 97). The applicant must be willing to provide documentation of the viability of the business (or proposed business in the form of a business plan), as well as be able to prove exactly where the capital they are investing originated, even if it is a gift. The capital cannot be drawn from the proceeds of criminal activity. Applicants must also show that they are in the process of investing and/or spending money in the United States on the business as of the time of the E-2 petition submission.

This requirement can be satisfied by such activities as signing a lease for office space, purchasing equipment, undertaking a marketing plan, obtaining legal services, hiring staff, etc. It is not enough for an applicant to have money sitting in the bank waiting for approval. The applicant's investment must be "at risk," clearly and unequivocally, in correlation to the potential success of the proposed business. If the visa is denied, the applicant will lose whatever money has been spent on developing the business plan or purchasing the established business.

There is no minimum amount in currency or its equivalent that is required to apply for an E-2 visa. Common sense tells us that the higher the amount the investor is willing to risk, the stronger the application. In practice, more often than not, the amount is at least $100,000, often higher. USCIS simply requires that the investment be substantial. They don't define "substantial" by attaching a figure to it. By substantial, it must be enough of an investment that the applicant wants the business to succeed and will focus all of his/her efforts to that end.

An applicant's ability to hire U.S. workers also strengthens the application, but is not required. If the applicant is not the sole owner of the business and is in partnership with others, the applicant must contribute a large enough amount that, proportionate to the cost of the entire business, the loss risk is significant. There will of course be businesses that require a larger capital influx based on the nature of the goods or services they provide, so an E-2 classification won't be denied based solely on the dollar amount of the investment. A car dealership will require a lot more cash for inventory than a marketing agency, but both could be seen as viable businesses for E-2 classification purposes.

The E-2 classification seeks to approve motivated entrepreneur applicants who want to do more than scrape out a living in the United States. The classification requires that the investment *not* be marginal, such that if the business or enterprise has little hope of turning a profit within a reasonable amount of time, and having a beneficial economic impact beyond supporting the investor and his/her family, the chances of approval are slimmer. The business must be real, legitimate, legal, and viable. It must contribute to the American economy in a positive way. This doesn't necessarily mean that if the E-2 investor doesn't have a bulletproof plan to be in the black within a certain time period of arrival, he/she will be rejected. The application adjudicators realize that some businesses may take a few years to get off the ground. But the applicant must offer reasonable projections and a clear-cut plan to steer the business toward success. If the business is a startup, it must be ready to "open its doors" upon approval of E-2 status, according to the law.

It must be noted that, in reality, some businesses wait until the visa application is approved before being completely ready, but applicants can still prove that money is being spent toward the operations of said business. The startup cannot still be in the idea phase to qualify. If the treaty investor is purchasing an existing business, the documentation must show concrete plans for continued success and growth of the business.

Additionally, the source of funds for the investment must be legitimate and legal. Ideally, they will be from a U.S.-based bank account in the investor's name. The easier it is to show that the E-2 investment capital comes from a legitimate source, the fewer challenges this piece of the puzzle will potentially represent.

In some cases, an E-2 visa will be granted for a treaty investor employee, provided that it can be demonstrated that the employee is "essential" to the operations of the U.S. business. As such, if the treaty investor seeks to apply for E-2 status for an employee, the employee must also be a citizen of the same treaty nation as the investor. That employee must be proven to be a vital component to the success of the proposed business. This employee must either have a special skill set, relevant experience, or must serve in a managerial capacity, capable of running day-to-day operations and ultimately make important business decisions.

Applying for an E-2 Visa While in the United States

Similar to its sister visa, the E-1, a foreign national seeking E-2 status while in the United States can apply to change his/her status to E-2 by filing Form I-129 (Petition for a Non-immigrant Worker) with USCIS. They must be present in another lawful, current, non-immigrant status at the time. The filing fee for this application is $460 at the time of this writing, but as with the other visas, these fees change periodically. It is best to visit the Department of State website for up-to-date filing fees (visit https://travel.state.gov/content/visas/en/employment/treaty.html).

If the applicant satisfies the requirements and provides the requested documentation, he/she will be granted E-2 status for a two-year period. The applicant will also be required to include a statement (usually a written statement is sufficient) of his/her intent to return to his/her home country after the expiration of the E-2 visa and the conclusion of his/her U.S. business dealings; notably, this statement is also often included in the corresponding business plan that is submitted with the petition. This may seem odd since the idea behind the visa is to encourage the development of a successful business in the United States and investment in the economy, but this visa is still a non-immigrant visa and not to be viewed as a direct path to a green card. There is significant risk involved for the applicant, and if for some reason the enterprise is unsuccessful and the investment is lost, the person will not be allowed to stay lawfully in the United States in this status. Essentially, he/she must agree to return home if things don't work out as planned.

It must be noted that if applying directly with USCIS for a change of status to E-2, the initial approval is only for two years, and if the applicant has to travel outside of the United States for any reason, he/she will have to reapply at a U.S. consular post to regain entry into the United States. This can be inconvenient and somewhat nerve-wracking for applicants and families. An approved I-129 application will not just be rubber-stamped. The documentation will be scrutinized carefully, and the person will have to go through another application process and interview to be issued an E-2 visa. Because of this, applicants may choose to file for E-2 status at a U.S. embassy or consulate from the outset.

Applying for an E-2 Visa
at a U.S. Embassy or Consulate

Applying for E-2 treaty investor status while outside of the United States requires that an application be submitted online to the U.S. Department of State using a form DS-160 (for the investor) and an additional form DS-156E for an E-2 employee. The fee associated with this application is $205 at the time of this writing, but fees change periodically. It is best to visit the Department of State website for up-to-date filing fees (visit https://travel.state.gov/content/visas/en/employment/treaty.html).

There is no filing fee for the DS-156E. You can review the list of U.S. embassies and consulates at www.usembassy.gov. Their individual websites will detail the procedure for applying for E-2 treaty investor status. Every country has its own specific methods and requirements with regard to granting or denying the treaty investor visa. Each embassy or consulate has different waiting periods to secure an interview, and each also has its own idea of what constitutes a substantial investment and a non-marginal/viable business. There is no across-the-board guarantee of approval and what works in one consulate may very well fail in another. Some countries are simply stricter in their scrutiny of the applications (see Chapter 11 for information regarding differences in business plan requirements). There may also be an additional issuance or "reciprocity" fee that is separate from the application fee in certain countries. To discover whether a specific country requires an additional fee, visit https://travel.state.gov/content/visas/en/fees/reciprocity-by-country.html.

A notable benefit to applying for E-2 status at an embassy or consulate is that, if approved, the treaty investor is granted entry for five years and can travel outside of the United States and back without restriction. Every five years, the E-2 visa is renewable indefinitely as long as a viable business and a substantial investment by the applicant continue.

Another benefit to entering the United States as an E-2 non-immigrant worker is that spouses of E-2 aliens are permitted to work while in the United States, and children of E-2 aliens under age 21 are permitted to attend school. The children of E-2 aliens under age 21 are not permitted to work. An E-2 spouse can obtain an Employment Authorization Document (EAD) and then apply for a social security number and a job with any company of his/her choosing.

TABLE 5.1. E-2 VISA STATISTICS BY TREATY NATION*

TREATY NATION	YEAR	NUMBER OF E-2 VISAS ISSUED
Afghanistan	2013	1
	2014	0
	2015	2
Argentina	2013	310
	2014	536
	2015	595
Australia	2013	313
	2014	327
	2015	393
Belgium	2013	182
	2014	191
	2015	246
Canada	2013	2,609
	2014	2,590
	2015	2,615
Colombia	2013	220
	2014	322
	2015	393
Egypt	2013	41
	2014	67
	2015	107

France	2013	2,218
	2014	2,641
	2015	3,248
Germany	2013	3,811
	2014	3,731
	2015	4,321
Israel	2013	37
	2014	39
	2015	44
Italy	2013	1,173
	2014	1,404
	2015	1,926
Japan	2013	11,333
	2014	11,439
	2015	12,172
Mexico	2013	3,001
	2014	2,707
	2015	2,580
Poland	2013	53
	2014	103
	2015	101
Spain	2013	1,299
	2014	1,480
	2015	1,946

Thailand	2013	320
	2014	427
	2015	506
Turkey	2013	244
	2014	422
	2015	371
United Kingdom	2013	2,488
	2014	2,915
	2015	2,935
Venezuela	2013	124
	2014	196
	2015	456

Data provided by the U.S. Department of State. Not all treaty nations are included.

The Path to Permanent Residence

An E-2 visa is classified as a non-immigrant visa, which means that it does not offer a direct path to permanent residence. However, there are a few indirect routes that put applicants on the path to permanent residence, whether as entrepreneurs or not. Because the E-2 visa is renewable indefinitely, permanent residence is not necessary as long as the applicant can prove his/her business is still viable and he/she is still investing substantial capital at personal risk.

An E-2 investor does not have to stay in the same business as the original application outlined. If one business fails, but the investor has ideas for another business and the capital to back it up, he/she can reapply for an E-2 based on this new venture. This person is also free to return to his/her home country at any time. For some, this is an ideal arrangement. For other E-2 treaty investors, as time goes on, they make the decision to immigrate to the United States and therefore seek an alternative path to obtaining a green card.

As mentioned earlier, one avenue toward this goal is to change status to that of an EB-5 investor. Because of its complexity, this status will be discussed in detail beginning in Chapter 8. Notably, in the author's experience, transitioning from an E-2 to an EB-5 has become an increasingly popular option over the recent few years. Approval for EB-5 translates to permanent residence for the investor and his/her family.

One of the many catalysts to an E-2 investor transitioning to an EB-5 is that the investor's children age out and are no longer covered by the investor's E-2 visa once they reach age 21. If the investor transitions to an EB-5 immigrant investor visa well enough in advance of the child(ren) reaching age 21, the children could then be covered by the parent's petition and could obtain independent permanent resident status that would remain intact after reaching age 21. Another catalyst is the investor's desire for permanence in his/her stay in the United States and ability to run his/her business without interruption, which can only be achieved through permanent residence. Other reasons include the possibility that the investor always intended to seek permanent residence but either lacked sufficient capital initially or was unwilling to wait for the extended processing period for the approval of the I-526, and used the E-2 option as a springboard.

Another avenue is to secure employment with a company willing to sponsor an H-1B specialty occupation visa and following that path to permanent residence. This, of course, would mean giving up ownership of the E-2 investor's business, but the experience of running a business is all consuming, and some applicants might welcome the opportunity to work in a corporate setting. Additionally, if the E-2 investor's spouse is able to find a job as an H-1B specialty occupation worker, that spouse can follow the path to permanent residence, and sponsor his/her spouse and children.

In the family-based category of immigrant visas, nothing is stopping an unmarried E-2 visa holder, or the holder of any other visa for that matter, from marrying a U.S. citizen, which, provided that it is a real, *bona fide* marriage, is the most certain avenue to permanent residence. Although this permanent residence path is always an option, it is not covered in this guide as it is neither employment nor business-related in nature.

When all is said and done, the E-2 treaty investor non-immigrant visa is an outstanding option for a motivated and savvy entrepreneur who has the capital to start and/or purchase a business in the United States. While the document requirements can seem daunting (see the E-2 document checklist herein), the end result is a potentially long-lasting, mutually beneficial, and lucrative opportunity for treaty nationals to live and work in the United States.

REAL-LIFE E-2 SCENARIOS

Various E-2 application examples can be used to illustrate the types of business investments that could potentially lead to a successful E-2 petition. These real-world examples can be referenced as invaluable tools in assessing what may constitute a "substantial investment" and a "viable business" that is not deemed "marginal." However, we must bear in mind that the granting—or denial—of an E-2 petition involves significant discretion coupled with a qualifying scenario.

Scenario 1

Mr. Z is hoping to buy a business in the United States using money he has earned over his career as an entrepreneur in Argentina. He has been visiting the United States on a B-1 business visitor visa with the intent of viewing some carwashes he hopes to purchase. While in the United States, he finds the perfect carwash with a purchase price of $250,000. The business is doing well and has a steady stream of customers, but Mr. Z feels he can grow the business significantly because of its location and begins to prepare his plans for growth. Before returning to Argentina, he puts down a retainer to engage the services of an immigration law firm to begin the E-2 application process and shows proof of $275,000 in cash in savings in Argentina available for wire transfer.

Mr. Z hires a commercial real estate agent to negotiate the terms of the purchase on his behalf. He also engages the services of a local marketing agency to begin a multimedia advertising blitz ready to be launched if his E-2 visa is approved. When he returns to Argentina, he works hard to prepare all of the necessary documentation to present to the embassy in Buenos Aires, and when he has consulted with his U.S. immigration attorney and feels ready to proceed, he submits his DS-160 online and schedules an interview with the embassy. His application is approved that day at the interview, and within a few weeks, he has entered the United States in E-2 status and is ready to take over and run the carwash.

Scenario 2

Mrs. R has been a successful hotel owner in Ireland for the past twenty years and is interested in spending some time in the United States to live and work closer to her grown children who have both emigrated. After searching online and consulting with her children, as well as visiting the United States to find a business for purchase, Mrs. R has found the perfect motel for sale that includes an owner apartment where she can live while she runs the day-to-day activities of the business.

The selling price of the motel is $800,000, and Mrs. R is able to put down $480,000 in cash and is hoping to finance the rest of the purchase price. In her detailed business plan, she outlines her steps toward growth, including the hiring of more local staff and plans for upgrades to the units to give the property a significant makeover.

Her son is a real estate agent who negotiates the purchase of the property while Mrs. R returns to Ireland to prepare her application for E-2 status. She secures financing for the remaining 40 percent of the purchase price and submits her completed DS-160 online and makes an appointment with the embassy in Dublin. After her interview, she is notified within two weeks that her E-2 visa has been approved, and she finalizes her plans to move to the Unites States to run her motel.

E-2 DOCUMENTATION CHECKLIST

Some consulates and embassies have additional unique requirements and interpretations. Some of these differences are discussed below. An E-2 applicant must check the website of the consulate or embassy through which he/she is applying to make sure all of the required documentation can be provided.

APPLICATION FORM (SAME AS E-1, SEE P. 71)

EVIDENCE OF OWNERSHIP AND NATIONALITY OF BUSINESS (SAME AS E-1)

EVIDENCE OF INVESTMENT IN THE UNITED STATES: E-2 APPLICATION ONLY

a) Substantiation of value of the enterprise.

b) Evidence of ownership of the funds invested.

c) Evidence of actual investment of funds in the enterprise, e.g., bank transfers, bank statements, escrow agreements.

d) Copies of mortgages, loan agreements, promissory notes.

e) Documentation of ownership of other company assets, e.g., equipment, inventory.

EVIDENCE OF REAL AND OPERATING ENTERPRISE IN THE UNITED STATES (E-2 APPLICATION ONLY)

a) Copies of most recent U.S. income tax return.

b) Copies of most recent audited financial report of balance sheet.

c) Business plan (Please see Chapter 11 for further information regarding Business Plans).

EVIDENCE ENTERPRISE IS MORE THAN MARGINAL (E-2 APPLICATION ONLY)

a) Copies of most recent personal and business U.S. income tax returns.

b) Copies of W-2 forms for employees.

c) Documentation of income from outside sources.

ADDITIONAL DOCUMENTATION FOR E-1/E-2 EMPLOYEE VISAS (SAME AS E-1)

ADDITIONAL DOCUMENTATION FOR DEPENDENTS (SAME AS E-1)

E-2 INFOGRAPHICS

E-2 NON-IMMIGRANT VISAS
(TREATY INVESTOR)

The E-2 (Treaty Investor) nonimmigrant visa is tailor-made for foreign nationals who are interested in starting or taking over a business in the U.S., provided they meet the criteria.

 If the alien applicant is a citizen of one of the nations with which the U.S. has a Treaty of Friendship, Commerce and Navigation, (s)he may be eligible for E-2 classification.

 The E-2 treaty investor visa requires a substantial investment of capital in a viable business in the U.S. with significant risk to the applicant. Substantial investment is not specifically defined, and depends on the actual business type and model.

 The alien applicant's intent must be to direct or run the business while they are in the U.S. on a temporary basis (must plan to return to home country upon expiration of the visa; however, unlimited renewals are available if conditions continue to be met).

This visa is an outstanding option for a motivated and savvy entrepreneur who has the capital to start and/or run a business in the U.S.

REQUIREMENTS FOR AN
E-2 VISA

 The alien applicant must be a national of a treaty nation.

 Certain investment requirements must be met before USCIS will grant the visa (substantial investment – not definitive – somewhat discretionary).

 The applicant must be willing to provide documentation of the viability of the business, as well as be able to prove exactly where the capital they are investing originated.

 Applicants must also show that they are in the process of investing and/or spending money in the U.S. on the business as of the time of the E2 petition submission.

E-2 FAQS

Q: How do I know I qualify for an E-2 visa?

A: If the visa applicant is a citizen of one of the seventy-eight eligible treaty countries, he/she qualifies for an E-2 visa. (Visit https://travel.state.gov/content/visas/en/fees/treaty.html for a complete list of all qualifying E-1 and E-2 treaty countries.) In addition, the business must be at least 50% owned by nationals from the applicant's home treaty country.

Q: What are the benefits of applying for an E-2 visa over an L-1 visa or and EB-5?

A: Applying for an E-2 visa is significantly less expensive and the application process is much faster than with an EB-5 or other green card process (and some foreign nationals would prefer not to become permanent U.S. residents for tax and other reasons), and unlike the L-1 visa, which limits the applicant's time in the United States, an E-2 visa can be renewed an indefinite number of times, provided that the criteria continue to be met.

Q: What qualifies as a substantial investment for an E-2 visa?

A: While there is no required minimum investment, an investment of $100,000 or greater is recommended. This investment must be at risk and is dependent upon the success of the business.

Q: How much will an E-2 visa application cost?

A: If done correctly the first time around (hiring a qualified team of knowledgeable and experienced experts will make the difference), the applicant can generally expect at an expenditure of anywhere from $14,000 to $25,000 as of the writing of this book (depending on the complexity and nature of the business, the professional team members selected, and specific visa qualifications, which can vary on a country-by-country basis) for the legal and business plan components of the process.

Q: What happens if the business fails?

A: The business must become self-sustaining within its first five years of operation, which will need to be clearly demonstrated within the business plan. If the visa holder can demonstrate that the business is successful as the visa expiration date approaches, the holder can apply for an E-2 visa renewal. If the business fails within the first five years, the visa will become invalid and the holder has an obligation to leave the United States immediately, even if the visa has not yet expired. Whether the holder actually departs in the event that the business is failing is not certain, and the enforcement of this requirement remains lax.

Q: What is required for an E-2 application?

A: The applicant is required to make a *substantial investment* into a new or existing U.S. enterprise and intend to direct said enterprise while residing in the United States. The applicant must document the *viability of the business,* as well as demonstrate the legality of the investment funds' origins. Appropriate forms, together with supporting documents and a business plan (in most cases), must be filed with USCIS or the relevant consulate, depending on which processing option is selected.

Q: What professionals do I need to hire for a successful application?

A: An experienced immigration attorney is a must, as is a qualified business plan professional with experience writing business plans that correspond to USCIS's requirements. Note that business plans for visa purposes are quite different from those prepared for capital-raising or other purposes, which is why an experienced professional or professional team is so highly recommended (see Chapter 12). A single-point-of-contact team to "quarterback" the entire application process is also highly recommended. This "quarterback" will oversee all of the components of the case, from legal petition to business plan and everyone in between, ensuring a pain-free, cost-effective, and efficient experience. For more information on the importance of a single-source quarterback, see Chapter 12.

Q: Can I renew my E-2 visa?

A: Yes, it is possible to renew an E-2 visa once every one, three, or five years, depending on reciprocity, but the renewability of an E-2 visa is contingent upon the success of the business. The applicant must prove that the business continues to satisfy the conditions of the E-2 visa to remain in the United States. As long as the visa holder continues to meet the visa requirements, he/she can renew the E-2 visa indefinitely.

CHAPTER 6

H-1B (Specialty Occupation Employment-Based Visa)

"The wealth of a country is in its working people."

—THEODORE HERZL,
FOUNDING MEMBER OF THE STATE OF ISRAEL

Among the group of visas classified as "non-immigrant," the employer-sponsored H-1B visa has unique elements. When an employer seeks to employ a foreign worker (the "petitioner") and when the foreign worker seeks entry into the United States as an H-1B applicant (the "beneficiary") or seeks a change of status to H-1B if already in the United States under another visa status, it is not uncommon for him/her to begin a quest for permanent residence almost immediately, perhaps even as the H-1B petition is pending.

That is because, somewhat contradictorily, an H-1B visa is one of the non-immigrant visas that permits "dual intent." Even though an H-1B visa is granted for a finite period of time, if an H-1B worker hopes to stay in the United States permanently, he/she can take the necessary steps toward that goal even while under this temporary status. In other words, this applicant does not have to have the sole intent of staying in the United States only temporarily. Their goal can be to immigrate.

H-1B status is granted for up to a total of six years (three years initially, with one renewal of another three years), so if a foreign worker hopes to remain permanently, he/she should begin the process as soon as is feasible. This process to become a permanent resident in most cases involves a process known as a Labor Certification. This will be discussed in more detail in Part Two of this book.

Prior to that, of course, there are very specific requirements to fulfill to be considered a qualified H-1B applicant, and there are very specific processes to follow prior to being granted an H-1B visa. Unlike the E and L visa categories, there is a cap on the number of new H-1B visas issued every year in the United States. This cap is 65,000 H-1Bs issued with an extra 20,000 available for applicants with advanced degrees from U.S. institutions.

As you can imagine, that cap is reached within days, making the H-1B a very competitive visa and causing frustration for large H-1B employers and prospective employees alike. who can't fill those H-1B eligible jobs. The window to file the application is tight, and there is a sense of randomness about the process that keeps applicants on edge.

Indeed, it *is* a lottery! USCIS begins accepting H-1B petitions on April 1 of each year and only for the first five business days of April. For those petitions subject to the H-1B cap, a computer picks which ones will be approved. A foreign worker sponsored by his/her employer for an H-1B eligible position can meet all of the requirements, but if his/her application arrives after the cap has been reached (again, usually within days of April 1 filing commence-ment), that person is out of luck. The H-1B visa will not be granted, and the employee will have to find an alternative way to enter and work legally in the United States until the following April, when they can repeat the process and try again. To put the competition in perspective, USCIS received 236,000 H-1B applications (remember the cap is 65,000) within the first five days of April 2016.

There are also other aspects of the H-1B program that make it controversial and bring it to the forefront of the ongoing immigration debate. Some argue that H-1B eligi-ble jobs could and should be filled by American workers. Some claim that American workers are displaced and even let go in favor of less experienced, and therefore less costly, foreign workers. In some instances, American workers are asked to train their H-1B replacements. H-1B eligible jobs only require a bachelor's degree or its equivalent, and they are not always so specialized that no worker in this country can be found for them, but yet they are issued for such nonspecialized jobs.

The immigration debate in the United States is com-plex, to say the least, and divides many in this country. But the rules are there for everyone to see, and if a for-eign applicant follows procedure and is approved and issued a visa to work in this country legally, then that ruling must be respected. Chances are, however, there will always be debate.

It must be mentioned that there are cap exemptions available to certain applicants, for instance H-1B transfers (they are in H-1B status and transfer to another H-1B eligible job) and non-profit researchers. An H-1B eligible worker with a master's degree or its equivalent is not subject to the 65,000 cap, but has an additional 20,000 granted for advanced degrees, as mentioned above. However, once the first 20,000 advanced degree H-1Bs have been issued, the remaining applicants go in with the regular 65,000. Because of these many complexities, in addition to seeking legal counsel for filing of the petition itself, it is also a good idea to seek legal counsel to see if perhaps a specific H-1B employer, job, or applicant might possibly be cap-exempt or even if there is an H-1B alternative.

Interestingly, there are subsections of the H-1B program that are reserved for specific countries and occupations. The H-1B1 reserves 6,800 visas for Chile and Singapore, with 1,400 for Chile and 5,400 for Singapore. If workers from these countries do not apply for these visas, the remainder of the 6,800 goes back in the pool of other H-1B applicants. Additionally, there are H-1B2 visas reserved for government project researchers and H-1B3 visas reserved for fashion models of distinction. What seems like a straightforward non-immigrant employer-sponsored finite work visa becomes something quite different upon closer examination!

The very first thing a potential H-1B applicant must have is a job offer from an U.S. employer willing to sponsor his/her visa. The applicant must hold a bachelor's degree (or its equivalent) or higher and the degree must be directly relevant to the work the applicant will be doing in the offered position. In other words, the job must require a specific degree or training for any potential hire, foreign or U.S. citizen. In theory, the purpose of the H-1B visa program was to attract skilled immigrant labor to the United States and to help fill jobs for which qualified U.S. workers could not be reasonably found. This came about as a result of the technology boom that began about twenty-five years ago and meant an explosion of jobs and a scarcity of skilled labor to fill them.

As people began to rely more and more on computers and technology for professional and personal communication, businesses found that they had thousands of jobs to fill. Companies such as Microsoft and Intel exploded, and there were not enough U.S. computer programmers to fill them. The H-1B program grew out of this need and the desire to populate the U.S. workforce with highly skilled immigrant labor.

Once a potential H-1B candidate finds a job with a company that is willing to sponsor his/her visa, the candidate must fill out the proper paperwork and be very mindful of dates and deadlines. A new year for H-1B's is in accordance with the government's fiscal calendar that begins on October 1 each year. The new "batch" of H-1B visas is not issued before then. In addition, each piece of the application puzzle carries its own deadlines and requirements, discussed next.

The Labor Condition Application

A prerequisite and first step *after* receiving a qualified job offer for approval of an H-1B visa is the filing of Department of Labor Form ETA-9035, known as the

Labor Condition Application (LCA). This form is an essential first step where employers are given the opportunity to provide information about themselves as well as the job they are offering the alien applicant, including salary to be paid, the employment period, and the location of the job. The employer must also make certain "attestations" or promises regarding the job. Note: LCA is not to be confused with a PERM certification—LCA is specific only to the H-1B visa and must be filed by the prospective employer.

These attestations are as follows: 1) the foreign worker will be paid the prevailing wage or the actual wage, whichever is higher (the Department of Labor itself can provide this information through statistical data), 2) employment of the foreign worker will not adversely affect U.S. workers similarly employed (hours, shifts, vacation time, benefits, etc.), 3) there is no strike or lockout affecting the position that the foreign worker will fill, and 4) the employer has notified the collective bargaining representative (if any) or similarly employed workers of its intent to fill the position with an H-1B alien (usually through posting in a public area of the company for ten business days).

The reason for demanding these promises from employers was to protect U.S. workers and jobs. It is also a foreshadowing of the Labor Certification that will be required for the H-1B visa applicant to receive permanent U.S. residence if they apply for it. The Department of Labor must be satisfied that U.S. workers aren't being fired or displaced and substituted with foreign labor for the bottom-line benefit of corporations.

The LCA is filed with the Department of Labor

electronically through the iCERT portal (https://icert. doleta.gov/) with supporting documentation, but only six months prior the proposed H-1B employee start date, and not before. There are a few exceptions made for these deadlines as well as a few exceptions allowing paper copies to be filed, one of them being a proven disability and another being the inability to apply electronically because of a lack of access.

To bypass electronic certification, applicants must receive advance permission. A Labor Condition Application that meets the above requirements and is filed in a timely fashion is approved usually within two weeks, and this approval is known as a "certified" LCA. USCIS will not accept Form I-129 (Petition for a Non-immigrant Worker) for an H-1B employee *without* a Labor Certification.

Filing Form I-129
(Petition for a Non-immigrant Worker)

Once a certified LCA is in hand, the petitioner (in the case of an H-1B visa, it must always be an employer) can file Form I-129 on behalf of the H-1B applicant. At the time of this writing, the fee for filing this petition is $460, but fees have a tendency to change and there can be a number of add-on charges such as premium processing, fraud prevention and detection, among others. A helpful checklist for H-1B filings can be found at www.uscis.gov (visit https://www.uscis.gov/sites/default/files/files/ form/m-735.pdf).

At the filing of the I-129 petition, the employer must provide supporting documentation to prove that the position they are offering qualifies as a specialty occupation. This includes proving that the position requires, at a minimum, a bachelor's degree or its equivalent in order to perform the duties required. If by chance the candidate does not have the equivalent of a U.S. bachelor's degree but is still being offered the job, the employer must prove that he/she has some sort of relevant training, specialized knowledge, or advanced certification that essentially acts as the equivalent of a degree.

Change of Status vs. Consular Processing

Once the I-129 petition has been approved, the H-1B applicant who is already in the United States under another lawful status (commonly an F student visa completing specialized studies) receives a change of status to H-1B via mail.

For foreign nationals applying for a job in the United States who are still living abroad, when the employer notifies them of the approval of the I-129 petition, the beneficiary can make plans to visit a U.S. embassy or consulate to officially receive the H-1B visa. They are not applying for a change of status in the United States; they are applying for an H-1B visa stamped directly in their passport. This has different requirements than those of a foreign worker already in the United States in another status.

The process required to receive an H-1B visa stamp from a U.S. consulate abroad must include specific documentation for consular processing. Along with the I-129 petition approval notice (known as an I-797), the applicant must complete a DS-160 (non-immigrant visa application) online through the U.S. Department of State. They must also furnish a valid passport, a color photo, resume, and transcripts, and a copy of the H-1B petition packet that was filed on their behalf by their employer sponsor.

When the consular processing is complete, the beneficiary can make arrangements to come to the United States. At their particular point of entry, the U.S. Customs and Border Protection will once again scrutinize their documentation. If approved, they will be issued an I-94 entry document, granted lawful entry in H-1B status, and can begin employment. It is important to understand that an approved I-129 does not guarantee entry into the United States. It will happen without incident in most cases, because the documentation supports the fact that proper procedure was followed, but again, it is not a guarantee.

Dependents of H-1B Workers

H-1B workers can bring their spouses and dependents into the United States, and while here, those dependents are in H-4 status. For the H-4 spouse, this status does not give employment authorization. This can be seen as a disadvantage for some families; however, once in the United States, the H-4 dependent can apply for a separate H-1B visa or another type of visa that will permit lawful employment in the United States. Additionally, as of May 2015, certain spouses in H-4 status have been authorized to apply for employment authorization if their H-1B spouse is well into the Labor Certification process on their way toward permanent residence. Of course, children in H-4 status under age 21 are able to attend school.

Benefits and Limitations of H-1B Visas

The H-1B visa is job-specific and job-dependent. If a candidate remains with the same employer for the first three-year stay and then extends his/her H-1B for the final three-year term, again with the same employer, he/she can be optimistic that this employer will see this employee through to an adjustment of status by sponsoring their Labor Certification and supporting the bid for permanent residence.

The Labor Certification application is a process that involves the sponsoring employer asserting to a greater extent that this job cannot be filled by anyone other than the foreign worker, and all attempts to find another suitable U.S. worker candidate have been unsuccessful. This must all be documented (including advertising the position at online job sites and in newspapers). In addition, any suitable U.S. worker candidates who seem qualified on paper must be interviewed. Valid reasons must be given for why the candidates who applied for the position are not qualified for the position. This is all part of the documentation process required to complete a successful Labor Certification application. An H-1B in a stable job for which they are singularly qualified can feel confident that his/her job is safe and the path to permanent residence is probable.

However, all jobs are subject not only to performance but also to corporate fit and economic fluctuations. An H-1B worker can lose his/her job just like anyone else and be out of status quickly and therefore not lawfully in the United States. This person must struggle to find another job with another employer willing to sponsor another job-specific H-1B visa. If unable to, he/she must return to his/her home country to either find work there, or begin the search for a new H-1B employer sponsor to begin the process over again. There are obvious drawbacks to this status.

Another drawback for the new H-1B applicant is the numeric cap of 65,000. A cap H-1B petition (in other words, an H-1B petition that is subject to the 65,000 cap and is not cap-exempt) can be filed perfectly and as advised during the first five business days in April just in time for the annual lottery distribution (the "lottery" is a computer-generated, random process of petition selection from the pool of all H-1B applicants, since there is a cap, although we remain unsure of the details or USCIS's methods); if approved, the H-1B officially commences on October 1 of each year, which is the fiscal start of USCIS's year), but if the petition is not filed timely within the April 1 window, that applicant is out of luck.

Some H1B Cap Exemptions and Other Special Cases

As with most aspects of U.S. immigration law, there are exceptions to every rule and special cases that make everything much more complex. Certain employers are not subject to the H-1B cap of 65,000, including non-profit research organizations, government research organizations, and institutions of higher learning. These employers can sponsor H-1B candidates at any time during the year.

There are also cap-exempt H-1B employees that include those foreign workers who are already in H-1B status and filing for an extension. In addition, a person will not be counted against the cap if he/she has already been counted within the past six years and is applying for the remaining portion of the six-year period of admission, unless he/she would be eligible for a new six years of H-1B status at the time the petition is filed.

A person could be eligible for a new six-year period if he/she was out of the country for one year or if the work was seasonal, intermittent, or less than six months per year. In some cases, if the person has not used all six years in H-1B status before leaving the United States, there could be an option to return to the United States for the unused time reaming (without becoming subject to the cap).

The first 20,000 H-1B applicants who qualify with a master's degree from a U.S. institution are also cap-exempt; their H-1B visas do not eat into the 65,000 available visas every year. However, if USCIS receives more than 20,000 master's cap petitions, USCIS usually conducts a lottery to select the 20,000 petitions.

There is one other cap-exempt, unique classification that needs to be mentioned. There is a unique subclassification of H-1B known as an H1B1. This visa is specifically for citizens of Chile and Singapore who receive a job offer in a specialty occupation from a U.S. employer. The Chile & Singapore Free Trade Agreement requires USCIS to exempt 6,800 visas from the H-1B visa cap, which are reserved collectively for eligible citizens of Chile and Singapore.

H-1B Controversy

There has been some controversy, as discussed, surrounding this non-immigrant visa status. This controversy has reached new heights under the Trump administration. Some argue that despite the requirements, some H-1B employers are displacing U.S. workers and seeking to hire younger foreign workers at lower wages. There are groups who are seeking immigration reform that would make this illegal, arguing corporations can't make a profit at the expense of U.S. workers.

For technical jobs, such as computer programmers, there was a time when there was a shortage of U.S. workers to fill these highly skilled positions. U.S. college graduates were simply not majoring in computer science at the rate necessary to stay aligned with technology. U.S. employers were forced to seek qualified candidates outside U.S. borders in order to conduct business. An influx of highly qualified workers from India and China, among other nations, entered on H-1B visas and filled those spots. The H-1B visa remains a controversial topic and it will continue to divide opinions for years to come.[1]

---

1. On April 18, 2017, the "Buy American and Hire American" executive order (EO) was signed by President Trump. This EO specifically directs various regulatory bodies to "as soon as practicable, suggest reforms to help ensure that H-1B visas are awarded to the most-skilled or highest-paid petition beneficiaries." Although this does not, of itself, change any of the H-1B laws, President Trump's concern with the H-1B program is being reflected through increased scrutiny. Other similar developments have been surfacing since Trump took office and will no doubt continue into the future unless and until his concerns can be overcome.

REAL-LIFE H-1B SCENARIO

Scenario

Ms. G has completed her studies in India and has received the equivalent of a U.S. bachelor's degree at Mumbai University in computer programming. Her dream is to work in the United States, eventually for good, and she chooses to go the H-1B route as an entry point for U.S. employment. She does her research and applies to various technology companies around the United States. She finds a technology company in Denver, Colorado, that is seeking employees with her skill set and qualifications, and she applies for the position.

She is hired in March, contingent on H-1B visa application approval. Her employer agrees to sponsor her H-1B and goes through the LCA process without incident, saving the public job position postings and other documentation to file with the Department of Labor. By April 2, they have a certified LCA and file a completed H-1B petition on Ms. G's behalf with everything in order. Her application is approved, as it is easy to see from the supporting documentation that Ms. G's job duties are highly skilled and technical and her services are greatly needed in this field.

On October 1, Ms. G waits anxiously for an I-797 from her employer that will allow her to enter the United States with an H-1B visa. The approval notice comes within a month, and she makes her arrangements at the U.S. embassy in Mumbai for entry into the United States. She files her DS-160 with supporting documentation, makes an appointment for an interview at the embassy, receives her approval that same day, and makes arrangements to enter the United States with an approved H-1B petition. She has no incident at customs in Denver and begins her journey as an H-1B worker living in the United States.

H-1B FAQS

Q: Is an immigration attorney necessary for an H-1B filing?

A: Although it is the H-1B employer's responsibility to file the LCA and I-129 petition with supporting documentation, the advice and assistance of a qualified immigration attorney can be key to the petition's success, although not a guarantee of it. An immigration attorney can help a candidate determine whether the job offer they have received is H-1B eligible, supervise the gathering and delivery of supporting documentation, and navigate filing deadlines and timing issues. They can assist in determining what fees will be required by the petitioning employer since there are many add-ons that must be included with the filing. They can also help determine whether a particular employer or position may be H-1B cap-exempt. This takes an intricate knowledge of immigration law, but can prove most beneficial for both the candidate and the employer by easing the stress accompanying the cap H-1B April lottery frenzy.

Q: Should an H-1B applicant travel while the visa is being processed?

A: It is recommended that an H-1B applicant not travel for the duration while their visa is being processed. (I experienced this firsthand as described in the preface to this book.) During the processing period, the applicant's status is considered to be in flux, and he/she has no official "status" in the United States until the H-1B visa is ultimately granted, unless he/she has an alternative visa status in the United States during said time. There is no doubt that this particular H-1B complexity faces increased scrutiny during the Trump administration.

Q: What is the difference between an H1-B visa and other temporary work visas?

A: Unlike other non-immigrant visas, such as the E-2 and L-1 visa, H1-B visas are restricted to yearly quotas—65,000 per fiscal year—and all applicants are subject to a lottery that takes place once a year, during the first five business days of April. An extra 20,000 H1-B visas are available per year, but only for applicants with a master's degree or higher in an area related to their occupation. However, once the first 20,000 advanced degree H1-B visas have been issued, the remainder of applicants with a master's degree or higher become subject to the 65,000 visa cap and are entered into the same lottery as those applicants with bachelor's degrees or equivalent.

Q: What are the benefits of applying for an H1-B visa?

A: The application process for an H1-B is both cheaper and faster than the process for a permanent employment-based work visa, and because of its status as a dual intent visa, it is relatively easy to transition from an H1-B visa to an immigrant visa. Additionally, unlike its E-2 and L-1 temporary work visa counter parts, H1-B applicants are not subject to investment or ownership requirements, or limited to executive and managerial employees.

Q: *How do I know if I qualify?*

A: There are three standards an applicant needs to meet to qualify for an H1-B visa: 1) the applicant must have a bachelor's degree (or equivalent—three years of work experience is equal to one year's worth of education in that field; therefore, it is possible to qualify for an H1-B visa without holding a bachelor's degree) or higher in a field related to his/her occupation; 2) the applicant must have an employer willing to sponsor his/her visa; and 3) the applicant must intend to work in the United States in a "specialty occupation" position (typically a job position that requires a bachelor's degree or higher) relevant to his/her degree, and will earn a prevailing wage for his/her work performed in said position.

Q: *Are there stay restrictions on the H1-B visa?*

A: Yes. The visa is initially set to expire after three years, but it can be extended once for an additional three-year period for total stay of six years in the United States.

Q: *Can I bring my spouse and/or children?*

A: Yes. Once H1-B status has been obtained, the beneficiary's spouse and/or unmarried minor children (under age 21) may be granted temporary residency under the H-4 visa, which is valid for the entire duration of the stay of the H1-B visa holder. Additionally, under some circumstances, spouses of H1-B visa holders may also work in virtually any job in the United States, as long as they apply correctly through USCIS (for more details, visit https://www.uscis.gov/working-united-states/

temporary-workers/employment-authorization-certain-h-4-dependent-spouses).

Q: How much will my H1-B visa application cost?

A: Employers cover the cost of applying for an H1-B visa. This can be anywhere from roughly $5,000–$15,000 for the legal and government filing fees. This number is largely dependent upon the size of the company (businesses with more than twenty-five employees are subject to higher fee rates than those with twenty-five or fewer employees). Additionally, H1-B petitioners can pay an additional $1,225 premium processing fee, should they decide to expedite the process.

Q: How long is the H1-B visa application process?

A: The H1-B processing time varies on a case-by-case basis, but typically there is a three to six month turnaround for H1-B applications. But, for an additional fee of $1,225, the petitioning employer can expedite the process through premium processing. By submitting Form 1-907, in conjunction with the Form I-129 and the added fee, the petitioner is provided with the premium processing service, which guarantees a fifteen-day turnaround. In other words, within fifteen days of submitting the application, the petitioner will receive an approval notice, denial notice, or a Request for Evidence (RFE).

Q: Are there any travel restrictions on an HB-1 visa?

A: No. As long as the visa is current, the holder can travel freely.

ADDITIONAL NON-IMMIGRANT CATEGORIES

As noted at the outset of this guide, the contents hereof are not intended to be exhaustive. Below is a discussion of a couple of additional non-immigrant options.

O Visa Category

The O Visa is available for those who have demonstrated extraordinary ability in a particular field. It is very similar to the EB-1 visa, although much less stringent, and does not offer a direct path to permanent residence as does the EB-1. It is granted for a period of 1–3 years and is renewable in one-year increments thereafter. Additionally, unlike the EB-1 visa for which the applicant can self-petition, employers must petition on behalf of O-1 beneficiaries.

O-1A applicants possess extraordinary abilities in sciences, education, business, or athletics (often used for visiting Professors and athletes, for example); O-1B applicants are in the motion picture or television industry (this is a very common option for foreign actors wishing to work in the United States for a period of time); O-2 applicants are those that need to accompany the O-1 beneficiary as an integral component of specific performances or events.

Foreign Entrepreneur Parole Rule

The Foreign Entrepreneur Parole is not a visa, but rather a means of entrée to the United States if certain conditions are met at the time of application and continue to be met throughout the life of the stay in the United States. One of the reasons for not including an detailed explanation of the Foreign Entrepreneur Role elsewhere in this guide is based on a concern that the Trump Administration may well either terminate this option prior to its effective date (it was originally introduced in 2014, modified significantly in August 2016, effective July 17, 2017), delay its implementation, or discontinue it at some early point during its life if indeed it is implemented on schedule. There are many immigration-related changes that have already occurred, continue to occur, and are expected to occur in the future under President Trump, and as much as I wish I—or anyone for that matter—had a crystal ball to foresee these changes and anticipate their impact, that is simply not the case.

A Parole is not a visa. It is a discretionary permission enter the United States (and to travel during its term) for the applicant and his/her family. Additionally, up to three parolees may receive status for each entity established in the United States. The Rule will apply to foreign entrepreneurs that have established a startup business in America within the 5 years preceding the filing of the parole application. The startup business must show significant American funding and be able to demonstrate that there is a high likelihood of expedited growth and employment creation. To qualify, the parolee must show that they will "substantially assist the entity with the growth and success of its business", and must also show that he/she has at least a 10% ownership interest and maintains some equity interest throughout the parole period.

This Parole will be available for a period of up to 5 years (initially issued 30 months with the availability of a second 30 months provided that certain criteria are met including the creation of at least 5 jobs). The only way to secure Parole is through entry INTO the United States from a foreign country. The investment into the United States must also attract bona fide American investment of at least $250,000 within 18 months of applying OR must receive a minimum of $100,000 from a qualified governmental award or grant. It is possible in certain circumstances for the entrepreneur to provide other compelling evidence of the "substantial potential for rapid growth and job creation" if he/she is unable to substantiate the investment requirement (see https://www.federalregister.gov/documents/2017/01/17/2017-00481/international-entrepreneur-rule).

The Parole grant is discretionary in nature. Thus, it can be terminated at any time if the underlying business discontinues operations or is no longer providing a significant domestic public benefit. Additionally, while the future of the Foreign Entrepreneur Parole remains uncertain, so does the question of whether it will offer a path to permanent residence. Most believe that it will not offer such a path, and instead recommend that an EB-2 National Interest Waiver be pursued (see Chapter 7).

PART TWO

Immigrant Visas

For those foreign nationals hoping to come to the United States to live and work permanently, there are a variety of immigrant visa options available to them depending on their particular circumstances. This part of the guide covers several of these immigrant visas, including the coveted EB-5 visa, one of the newest ways to obtain a green card for qualified applicants who meet applicable investment and job creation requirements.

CHAPTER 7

EB (Employment-Based) Classifications

"In 2013, over 40 million foreign-born representing 13% of the population resided in the United States."[1]

—THE BROOKINGS INSTITUTION

The United States has always encouraged the legal immigration of foreign nationals who would come to this country and make significant contributions to our economy, our culture, and our way of life. To that end, the U.S. government defined several categories to be made available to qualified foreign nationals desirous of living and working permanently in the United States based on their profession or occupation.

Among this group of visas classified as employment-based immigrant visas, the EB categories (EB-1, EB-2, EB-3, EB-4, and EB-5) can potentially be the perfect choice for certain foreign workers who are deemed to

---

1. Dews, Fred. "What Percentage of U.S. Population Is Foreign Born?" Brookings. October 3, 2013. Accessed April 25, 2017. www.brookings.edu/blog/brookings-now/2013/10/03/what-percentage-of-u-s-population-is-foreign-born.

have extraordinary ability, exceptional ability, extensive specialized experience, advanced degrees, are immigrant investors generating jobs for U.S. workers, or fall into another type of special immigrant category. As with all other non-immigrant and immigrant work visas, these employment-based immigrant visas each have a specific set of requirements that must be backed up with the appropriate documentation.

A few of the EB categories require the filing of a PERM Labor Certification, while others do not. Some have faster processing times, while others face a significant backlog. This chapter briefly discusses the EB classifications and gives an overview of the PERM process, while ultimately focusing on the EB-2 (National Interest Waiver), an immigrant visa that does *not* require a PERM application. (Note: Due to its complexity, the EB-5 immigrant investor visa will be discussed beginning in Chapter 8.)

EB-1 Immigrant Visa

The EB-1 immigrant visa is reserved for foreign nationals who possess an *extraordinary ability,* and/or are outstanding professors or researchers, or are multinational executives or managers. Essentially, this visa is reserved for those foreign nationals who have risen to the top of their chosen profession and are acknowledged as such within that profession and beyond.

The word "extraordinary" in and of itself possesses an almost magical quality, which can be somewhat deceiving in this case. To qualify, the applicant must possess *at least three of the ten criteria listed by USCIS.* These criteria include those outlined in the infographic below:

EB-1 EXTRAORDINARY ABILITY INFOGRAPHIC

EB-1

This visa is perfect for foreign nationals who are able to demonstrate an extraordinary ability, are outstanding professors or researchers or are multi-national executives or managers.

If a candidate can be shown to have extraordinary ability in their chosen field, they do not need an employer sponsor (that is a job offer) and they do not require an approved PERM Labor Certification in order to obtain their green card. Extraordinary ability requires at least 3 of these criteria:

- Prizes or awards for excellence in their field
- Membership in prestigious associations
- Published material about the applicant in major publications
- Evidence of having been asked to judge the work of other professionals in their field
- Original contributions of major significance (such as patents)
- Publication of their own work in scholarly journals, major media or trade publications
- For artists, evidence of exhibits
- Leadership roles in prestigious organizations
- A high salary in relation to other professionals in the field
- For performing artists, evidence of commercial success

These criteria clearly reflect the superior level of applicant required for a successful EB-1 extraordinary ability petition. For a real-world example, an Academy Award–winning actress or Nobel Prize winner would be a shoo-in for an EB-1, as would Mark Zuckerberg, Steve Jobs, Steven Spielberg, or Walt Disney. Because of the requirements, this visa is difficult to obtain and the burden of proof is high. However, if a candidate can be shown to have extraordinary ability in his/her chosen field, he/she does not need an employer sponsor (that is, a job offer) and does not require an approved PERM Labor Certification to obtain a green card. Instead, EB-1 candidates are given first preference, and the processing time is faster than most other visas. If there is a real possibility of success in an EB-1 case, it is most certainly the quickest and least expensive path to permanent residence!

Other potential candidates for an EB-1 are outstanding professors or researchers. In this EB-1 category, the applicant must have a job offer from a U.S. employer for a tenure track teaching or comparable research position with at least three years of prior teaching experience. Some of the other requirements are at least two of the following:

- Major prize or award for outstanding achievement in chosen academic field;

- Membership in prestigious organizations;

- Citations of applicant's work by others in the field;

- Evidence of having been asked to judge the work of another in the field;

- Original or scholarly research contributions in field of expertise; and

- Publication of their own work in internationally circulated scholarly journals.

The final EB-1 subcategory is a multinational executive or manager—EB-1(c)(3). This category requires the foreign national to have been employed outside the United States for at least one of the last three years by the same company that is extending the offer in the United States and sponsoring the petition (similar to the L-1 non-immigrant visa requirements outlined in Chapter 2). In this case, the company would be subject to scrutiny to ensure the likelihood of stability and longevity so as to support the proposed visa beneficiary for the duration of the visa period.

EB-2 Immigrant Visa

The EB-2 immigrant visa is similar to the EB-1 in that it is tailor made for professionals, but has slightly less stringent requirements. The EB-2 seeks applicants who hold advanced degrees or have exceptional (as opposed to extraordinary) ability in the arts, sciences, or business. For the EB-2 advanced degree applicant, a master's degree or equivalent is required (equivalent being a bachelor's with five years of experience in the field of expertise).

For the exceptional ability EB-2, USCIS seeks applicants who can prove that their ability and expertise are above what would be normally found in their chosen profession. To that end, they must meet three of the following criteria, with supporting documentation:

- Proof of a degree in the field of expertise;

- Proof of ten years of full-time experience in the chosen profession;

- License or certification to practice in the chosen profession;

- Proof of a salary commensurate with someone of exceptional ability and experience;

- Membership in a professional association;

- Proof of recognition in the chosen field by other professionals in the same field, government entities, or business/professional organizations; and

- Other comparable eligibility proof.

The EB-2 visa *does* require an approved PERM Labor Certification prior to filing the immigrant petition as mentioned earlier, unless the applicant can prove that granting him or her an EB-2 visa is in the national interest and therefore waive the PERM requirement. Before the EB-2 National Interest Waiver in discussed in detail, below is a brief outline of the PERM Labor Certification process.

PERM Labor Certification

Chapter 6 discussed the H-1B Labor Condition Application requirement, which was put in place to protect American and foreign workers from unfair wages, unsatisfactory working conditions, and discriminatory practices. PERM Labor Certification has the same essential purpose, that is, to protect U.S. and foreign workers, but because the foreign worker is applying for a permanent work visa, the steps taken to safeguard the integrity of the process are taken further.

The term PERM Labor Certification has been used since March 2005 when the forms used to file for permanent labor certification regarding a position being offered to a foreign national in the United States were changed by the U.S. Department of Labor (DOL). Prior to that, it was simply called Labor Certification. To try to make the process of filing electronically more efficient and streamlined, the DOL eliminated the prior form ETA 750 (used in the original Labor Certification) and replaced it with an ETA 9089, which is now commonly known as the PERM Labor Certification. Although paper filings are accepted, the DOL *strongly* encourages electronic filing of the PERM Labor Certification. There are no DOL fees for this filing at this time.

A helpful way of looking at the PERM Labor Certification is to view it as a test of the market. When an employer hopes to sponsor a foreign worker for a permanent job in the United States, that petitioning employer must prove, to the satisfaction of the DOL, that a qualified U.S. worker was not found for that same position despite reasonable efforts. The petitioning employer proves this by demonstrating these recruitment efforts. The DOL guidelines require that the petitioning employer advertise the position being offered to the foreign worker in a newspaper of general circulation for at least two Sundays as well as via online job boards, as well as with the appropriate state workforce agency and posting conspicuously within the company and on the company website.

All recruitment efforts must be well-documented, of course, since they will be part of the file submitted to the DOL in support of the PERM application. Any U.S. citizen/legal resident who applies for the advertised position whose applications seem qualified on their face must be interviewed. This process is time-consuming and stressful for both the petitioning employer and the foreign worker.

After all applicants have been reviewed and those seemingly qualified have been interviewed, the employer then needs to document why none of these applicants will be hired or the advertised position. They must also reiterate why the foreign employee/applicant is the only person qualified for the position. The employer is not *required* to hire any of the applicants interviewed, but for obvious reasons, a PERM application that includes a qualified U.S. citizen/legal resident applicant that was not hired is one that could be challenged or rejected by the DOL.

If, however, the petitioning employer is able to document to the satisfaction of the DOL that no qualified U.S. worker was found to fill the position, the PERM will be approved and the employer can then file a Form I-140 (Immigrant Petition for Alien Worker) and take the rest of the process back to USCIS to complete the final steps on the road to permanent residence.

Again, all of this is very time-consuming. A PERM can take up to six months or longer to be approved. For that reason, in addition to the extensive paperwork and extra stress, if a foreign applicant can find a way to *avoid* filing a PERM Labor Certification, such a course of action would be preferable. The EB-2 (National Interest Waiver) outlined next affords such an opportunity.

EB-2 National Interest Waiver (NIW)

The National Interest Waiver is exactly as the name suggests. The foreign applicant should be granted an EB-2 visa with a national interest waiver because doing so is in the national interest. First, they must meet the EB-2 exceptional ability criteria, as discussed earlier. But, in addition, they must prove the national interest component. But how can "national interest" be satisfactorily defined? What constitutes national interest? Interestingly, USCIS does not rely on statute or regulation to determine this. Instead, until 2016, USCIS looked to a 1998 Administrative Appeals Office (AAO) precedent decision called Matter of New York State Department of Transportation, 22 I&N Dec. 215. In 2016, the NYSDOT decision was abandoned and replaced by Matter of Dhanasar, 26 I&N Dec. 884 (AAO 2016) which sets out that USCIS may grant a National Interest Waiver if the petitioner is able to demonstrated:

1. that the foreign national's proposed endeavor has both substantial merit and national importance;

2. that he or she is well positioned to advance the proposed endeavor; and

3. that, on balance, it would be beneficial to the United States to waive the job offer and labor certification requirements. Matter of New York State Dep't of Transp., 22 I&N Dec. 215 (Acting Assoc. Comm'r 1998), vacated.

There is little doubt that the National Interest Waiver is a subjective decision made by USCIS adjudicator, but the criteria make it clear that it will be no easy task to have the National Interest Waiver granted, subjectivity aside. If this is the route the applicant chooses to take, he/she can file Form I-140 (Immigrant Petition for Alien Worker), and under "Part 2. Petition Type" can check the box (1.i.) requesting a National Interest Waiver.

With regard to fees, on December 23, 2016, USCIS raised the fees for all but a few of its forms. The I-140 fee was raised significantly, from $580 to $700. It is best to check USCIS website periodically to ascertain current fees for all of the required immigration forms (visit https://www.uscis.gov/forms/our-fees).

EB-3 and EB-4 Immigrant Visas

The remaining EB classifications to be briefly discussed in this chapter are the EB-3 and EB-4 classifications. The EB-3 certification requires an approved PERM Labor Certification and take a substantial amount of time to process even after (or if) the Labor Certification is approved. Because there are fewer requirements, these visa applications are less scrutinized by USCIS, but there is a backlog, and the wait for approval can be not just months, but years.

The EB-3 covers what are considered skilled workers, professionals (jobs that require a bachelor's degree), and other workers (unskilled), performing jobs that are not of a seasonal or temporary nature. The crux of the EB-3 is that the foreign national applicant will be performing a job for which qualified workers in the United States cannot be found.

There can be no escaping the Labor Certification process, and the risk is significant that a U.S. citizen (or green card holder) will apply and be qualified for the advertised position. Some examples would be mechanics or chefs. In the "other worker" categories, some examples would be nannies or housekeepers. Again, because these jobs don't require advanced degrees or exceptional ability, obtaining permanent residence through them can be an uphill battle.

The EB-4 covers religious workers, some translators, certain radio broadcasters, and a cross section of foreign nationals considered special immigrants. This category is small and somewhat esoteric, and covering it in any detail goes beyond the scope of this book.

Some employment-based immigrant visas offer hope to those foreign workers who not only possess many desirable qualities, but also have the full support of a U.S. employer who believes in their abilities and values their contributions enough to sponsor them throughout the green card process. This is a significant vote of confidence and an indication of the caliber of applicant entering the United States as an EB visa hopeful. While the "extraordinary" candidates (as defined by USCIS) may be few and far between, there is certainly a signif-icant amount of applicants holding advanced degrees and working at a very high level in their chosen field.

For the EB-5 immigrant investor, the bar is set high as well, but as you will learn in the next chapter, with the approval of EB-5 petitions comes the corresponding boost to the U.S. economy and significant contributions across the board.

EB INFOGRAPHIC

EMPLOYMENT - BASED CATEGORIES

EB-2

 The EB-2 is suitable for applicants who hold advanced degrees or have exceptional ability in the arts, sciences or business.

 For the EB-2 advanced degree applicant, a master's degree or equivalent is required (equivalent being a bachelor's with five years of experience in the field of expertise).

 It requires an approved PERM Labor Certification prior to filing the immigrant petition, unless the applicant can prove that granting him/her an EB-2 visa is in the national interest and therefore waiving the Labor Certification requirement.

EB-3 & EB-4

 Both of these classifications **require an approved PERM Labor Certification** and take a substantial amount of time to process even after (or if) the Labor Cert is approved.

 The **EB-3** covers what are considered to be skilled workers, professionals (jobs that require a bachelor's degree) and other workers (unskilled), performing jobs that are not of a seasonal or temporary nature.

 The **EB-4** covers religious workers, some translators, certain radio broadcasters and a cross section of foreign nationals considered special immigrants.

EB VISA FAQS

Q: What is an employment-based (EB) visa?

A: Employment-based immigration options provide an opportunity for foreign nationals who meet very strict requirements to immigrate to the U.S. as permanent residents (green card holders), and eventually to apply for U.S. citizenship. There are a total of approximately 140,000 EB visas available per fiscal year. The quota for all EB visas is distributed between the five different types of EB visas (EB-1, EB-2, EB-3, EB-4, and EB-5) each year, which often results in a backlog in processing times. The strictest quota is 10,000, which applies to the coveted EB-5 Immigrant Investor visa.

Q: What are the benefits of applying for an employment-based (EB) visa?

A: While the process to secure an EB visa can be a long, expensive, and arduous, this may be well worth the pain for those who qualify, as the end result is a permanent resident green card that paves the way to applying for eventual U.S. citizenship.

Q: What is the difference between an EB-1 visa and an EB-2 visa?

A: The major difference between an EB-1 visa and an EB-2 visa are the qualifications the petitioner must meet in order to apply. EB-1 visas, or first preference visas, are set aside for individuals with extraordinary ability (i.e., a Nobel Laureate or Pulitzer Prize winner or an applicant of similar stature), an outstanding professor or researcher, and/or a multinational executive or manager.

For an individual to qualify for an EB-1 visa, chances are he/she is on a similar level to the likes of Walt Disney, Bill Gates, or Steve Jobs, as mentioned earlier. On the other hand, an EB-2 visa, or second preference visa, while similar to the EB-1 visa, applies to foreign nationals with an exceptional ability, and/or an advanced degree. Petitioners applying for an EB-2 visa also qualify for a National Interest Waiver, which will allow them to skip the PERM Labor Certification portion of the application process. EB-1 visas, since they are first preference, are processed more quickly and efficiently than EB-2 visas, which as noted are in the second preference category.

Q: What qualifies as "extraordinary ability" (EB-1)?

A: USCIS defines "extraordinary ability" as, "sustained national or international acclaim." Applicants who qualify must provide documentation, such as awards, published materials, major contributions to an area of expertise, and/or commercial success. Foreign nationals most likely to qualify are Olympic medalists, Nobel Laureates, multinational executives, Oscar/Grammy/Emmy/Tony Award–winning performers, professionals that have achieved a significant level of notoriety or recognition in their field, acclaimed writers, developers of unprecedented technologies or systems, etc. Applicants must meet at least three of ten possible qualifications to satisfy the definition, as detailed previously.

Q: What qualifies as "exceptional ability" (EB-2)?

A: USCIS defines "exceptional ability" as, "a degree of expertise significantly above that ordinarily encountered in the sciences, arts, or business." The petitioner must provide at least three documents evidencing their exceptional ability, which could include records, licenses, awards, and recognitions.

Q: What is a National Interest Waiver (EB-2)?

A: The National Interest Waiver (NIW) applies to EB-2 visa petitioners only, and allows certain qualified applicants to waive the PERM Labor Certification portion of the application process because it is in the national interest for the applicant to get into the United States as soon as possible. An NIW also waives the standard EB-2 requirement for a permanent job offer to be in place prior to the application's submission.

Q: How does an applicant know if he/she qualifies for an EB-3 visa?

A: An EB-3 petitioner must have a permanent, full-time job offer from an employer in hand prior to submitting his/her application. The third preference visa is set aside for qualified professionals hired to do a job which requires a U.S. bachelor's degree or its foreign equivalent, skilled workers hired to do a job that requires at least two year of relevant training or work experience, and/or other workers hired to perform unskilled labor requiring less than two years of related training or work experience. All EB-3 petitioners are subject to the PERM Labor Certification program, which requires proof that there are no authorized U.S. workers available to fill the position.

Q: Who qualifies for an EB-4 visa?

A: The EB-4, or fourth preference visa, is set aside for "special immigrants," such as religious workers, certain physicians, Afghan and Iraqi translators, international employees of the U.S. government, etc., and their families.

Q: How long is the process for an EB visa?

A: The length of the process varies and is dependent on different factors, such as the particular visa type and the number of applicants per year. For example, an EB-1 first preference visa could take as little as a month or two, whereas EB-5 visa processing times can be twelve to eighteen months or even longer.

Q: How much will an EB visa potentially cost me?

A: Cost varies depending on the type of visa and the complexity of the case. The cost of applying for an EB visa ranges from roughly $15,000 to $50,000 in filing and legal fees.

REAL-LIFE EB SCENARIOS

Scenario 1 (EB-1)

Ms. T is a young Indian national and has been working as a professor of mechanical engineering at the Indian Institute of Technology Bombay (IITB) in Mumbai for the past three years. Growing up, Ms. T was an engineering child prodigy who graduated from Oxford University with a PhD in mechanical engineering at the age of 21. She returned to Mumbai shortly thereafter with a Nobel Peace Prize for her original work on clean energy solutions. During her time at IITB, she published numerous research papers and received international notoriety for her work.

Over the past few months, Columbia University has been shamelessly courting Ms. T to take up a position in their engineering department and even offered her automatic tenure. After careful thought and consideration, Ms. T decides to take Columbia University up on their offer, and they hire an immigration attorney to file an I-140 (Immigrant Petition for Alien Worker).

The attorney packages together the evidence of Ms. T's extraordinary ability as an outstanding researcher and professor, such as her Nobel Peace Prize, her articles published in journals with international acclaim, her original research contributions to the field of mechanical engineering, and articles about her work written by credible mechanical engineers and published in internationally recognized publications. The attorney submits Ms. T's petition to USCIS, and Columbia University pays the filing fees.

Upon reviewing her application, USCIS determines that Ms. T does indeed qualify for a first preference EB-1 visa and grants Ms. T a green card. Ms. T picks up and moves to her new apartment about a mile away from campus and begins her career as a professor at one of the top universities in the nation.

Scenario 2 (EB-2)

Mr. B is a French national and has been vice president of development at a large international clothing retail company for the past fifteen years. He has a master's degree in economics and a PhD in business management. Mr. B and his partner have always dreamed of starting fresh in the United States and have finally reached the point in their lives where they are ready to do just that. Mr. B recently patented a brand new and innovated marketing tool to help struggling retail businesses and already has a few, large American companies interested in retaining his services.

Mr. B retains a U.S. immigration firm in New York City to assist with his immigration plans. The attorneys advise Mr. B to apply for an EB-2 visa with a National Interest Waiver (NIW), as he meets all the qualifications and it is in the national interest to get him into the United States as soon as possible to help the struggling American corporations find success. Mr. B provides his attorneys with documentation evidencing his exceptional ability, such as letters documenting his fifteen years' experience in business development and management, academic records, and the various awards he has received in recognition of his achievements and contributions to the world of business development. He also arranges for a professional immigration business plan company to prepare a business plan to support his EB-2 petition.

Mr. B's attorneys file an I-140 NIW petition, supported by the professional business plan, with USCIS on Mr. B's behalf. Mr. B's application is approved shortly thereafter, and he and his partner sell their home in France and move to New York City to start a new and happy life as American residents.

Scenario 3 (EB-3)

Mrs. Q is an executive chef at a local American Restaurant in Bangkok, Thailand, where she creates amazing Thai-American fusion food. She received a bachelor's degree in culinary management as well as an associate's degree in culinary arts from the International Culinary Schools at the Art Institutes, San Francisco.

Mrs. Q loved California and decides that she wants to move back there with her family. Mrs. Q works most nights, but in the morning, while her children are attending school, Mrs. Q applies for as many executive chef positions in cities across California as she can find. After multiple Skype interviews and a brief trip to Los Angeles to showcase her work, she receives an offer from an American bistro restaurant in Los Angeles, which is looking to change things up and revamp their menu, and to open additional locations. Mrs. Q accepts the position and the restaurant owners hire a local immigration attorney who specializes in employment-based immigrant visas to handle Mrs. Q's EB-3 petition and PERM Labor Certification.

The process takes roughly a year and a half, but eventually, due to the comprehensive file and extensive proof provided, USCIS determines that there is no American employee available to serve in the position offered to Mrs. Q and her petition is finally approved. Having waited anxiously for this day to come, and almost having given up hope, Mrs. Q quickly relocates with her family to Los Angeles, and starts her career as the new executive chef for the restaurant, which has opened a second location.

CHAPTER 8

Demystifying the Mysterious EB-5 Visa

"Complexity is your enemy. Any fool can make something complicated. It is hard to keep things simple."

—SIR RICHARD BRANSON

• As of May 1, 2017, USCIS has approved a total of 880 regional centers;

• In Q1 2017 alone, the EB-5 program generated over $1.6 billion in capital. EB-5 has generated over $3.8 billion in foreign direct investment in FY2016 and the program has attracted over $16.8 billion in capital investment since 2008;

• Based on the latest study by the Department of Commerce, EB-5 projects in FY2012 and 2013 were expected to create over 174,000 American jobs—that is 16 jobs per EB-5 investor.

SOURCE: IIUSA (Invest In the USA)

The final business-oriented immigration visa to be discussed in this book is the EB-5 Immigrant Investor

Program, which is the only business visa that paves a *direct* path to permanent residence. Officially, the EB-5 visa is the employment-based fifth preference category of lawful permanent resident (green card) category, specifically the fifth preference employment-driven immigrant investor visa category.

The EB-5 visa gives foreign entrepreneurs and investors the opportunity to secure permanent residence for themselves and their immediate families for investments that correlate to stimulating the American economy based on a *significant* capital investment ($1 million or $500,000, at the time of this writing) in a *new commercial enterprise* and, with that investment, *creating or preserving (at least) ten full-time jobs* for U.S. workers.

Because of its complexity, EB-5 investment requirements and the application process are addressed over the next few chapters. Despite its complexity, the EB-5 Immigrant Investor Program is a sound option for foreign investors with access to significant capital who are seeking permanent residence, as well as U.S. businesses seeking alternative capital. The opportunity to be involved, whether actively or passively, in a substantial commercial enterprise that creates jobs and stimulates the economy is clearly a win-win scenario for all involved. With the right support and guidance throughout the process, potential EB-5 investors can successfully avail themselves of this immigration option and pursue the American Dream, while U.S. business owners and developers can access foreign investor capital to establish or expand their domestic businesses.

EB-5 Qualifications

The following are the overall EB-5 qualifications:

- Minimum investment of $1 million or $500,000 in a Targeted Employment Area (TEA);[1]

- Investment in a new commercial enterprise (NCE) created *after* 1990; and

- Investment must create (or preserve, in the case of a troubled business[2]) ten permanent full-time jobs for qualified U.S. workers[3].

The capital investment required by the foreign national is *currently* either $1 million or $500,000 (see below for further details). Note that these amounts are subject to change in the very near future, so please check USCIS website (www.uscis.gov) for updated information.

The lesser minimum is available to those foreign nationals whose investment is located in a Targeted Employment Area (TEA), that is, an area that is rural (outside a city of fewer than 20,000 people) or that suffers from significant unemployment (150 percent of the national average). A foreign national investing at

---

1. This amount is subject to change in the near future—stay tuned!

2. A *troubled business* must have operated for at least two years and has incurred a net loss of at least 20% of the business' net worth prior to the loss during the two years prior to the I-526 priority date.

3. Creating (or preserving) ten permanent full-time jobs is a minimum requirement; creating (or preserving) additional jobs is strongly recommended.

least $1 million can invest directly in a new commercial enterprise located *anywhere* in the United States or its territories. The three critical words are: *Location, Location, Location.* This is important because the *single* determinant of the minimum investment amount required to apply for an EB-5, no matter which path is pursued, is *location*—specifically, whether the EB-5 project/subject business is located in a TEA or outside of a TEA.

A key component to a successful EB-5 application is the identification of the right type of business into which to invest *and* a comprehensive business plan showing exactly how the business will be viable and how it will create and/or preserve ten full-time jobs for U.S. workers (the "preserving jobs" option is reserved for *troubled businesses,* which have their own unique set of criteria that are *not* being specifically addressed within the scope of this book). Some of the most popular types of businesses selected for EB-5 investment include hotels, franchises, restaurants, real estate developments, assisted living facilities, infrastructure projects, and technology companies. Essentially, any type of legal, for-profit business is *eligible* on its face, but not all businesses lend themselves to EB-5 for a variety of reasons, such as capitalization or the creation of ten full-time jobs. Choosing the right business is definitely the critical—and most important—first step.

History of the EB-5 Program

The EB-5 Immigrant Investor Visa Program was originally established by Congress in 1990 in an effort to stimulate

the U.S. economy through job creation and capital investment by foreign nationals. It was included in Congress's
Immigration Act of 1990. This Act significantly restruc-
tured the U.S. immigration system. It is administered by
USCIS and has been a generally successful and direct
route to permanent residence for qualified foreign investors with adequate investment capital.

When the EB-5 visa category was first created, only
the direct investment option was available. In 1992, the
Regional Center Program came into being as a "pilot
program," which means that it "sunsets," or otherwise is
set to discontinue, after a certain period. This program
allows for a $500,000 investment by an EB-5 applicant
into large projects in designated areas, most of which
fall within TEA locations. The Regional Center Program
was initially set up as a four-year program. A regional
center is essentially an economic entity designated by
USCIS to sponsor and be involved in raising capital for
EB-5 investments with the goal of promoting economic
growth and creating jobs. Regional centers promote
foreign investment, job creation, improved regional
productivity, and economic growth. As noted, most
regional centers are approved in TEA locations, thus
qualifying for the reduced investment requirement. By
pooling together resources (i.e., the EB-5 investors'
capital), regional centers can undertake large, multi-
million-dollar projects. They also give foreign investors
a "passive" investment option if they don't want to be
involved in the day-to-day running of a for-profit commercial enterprise, but want the immigration benefit of
their $500,000 investment.

Regional center owners must apply for designation with USCIS in order to work with EB-5 projects. To be designated as a regional center, a number of requirements must be initially met to the satisfaction of USCIS, and many must also be fulfilled on an ongoing basis. At one point, there were more than 1,270 approved regional centers, but efforts to shut down dormant or inactive regional centers continue to grow and the number decreased significantly to 880 as of March 2017. An ever-changing regional center list is available for review at the USCIS website (visit https://www. uscis.gov/working-united-states/permanent-workers/ employment-based-immigration-fifth-preference-eb-5/ immigrant-investor-regional-centers).

EB-5 Visa Quotas

USCIS currently sets aside 10,000 available EB-5 visas each year. These visas are secured through the filing of Form I-526 (Immigrant Petition by Alien Entrepreneur), together with all of the required documentation, including a comprehensive, detailed, compliant business plan.

Prior to 2014, the total number of EB-5 applications received was not even close to the quota. (Please see this link for details: https://www.uscis.gov/sites/default/ files/USCIS/Resources/Reports%20and%20Studies/ Immigration%20Forms%20Data/Employment-based/ I526_performancedata_fy2016_qtr4.pdf.) In 2014, this changed forever when USCIS received 10,923 EB-5 visa petitions, more than 8,000 of which were from Mainland China. That figure climbed steadily over the next two years, reaching 14,147 EB-5 visa petitions received in 2016.

With these figures rising, the importance of submitting an outstanding package, including an EB-5-compliant, comprehensive, and specific business plan to eventually support the individual investor's Form I-526, whether in a direct investment or regional center case, cannot be overstated. Another critical component includes meticulously documenting the source and path of the foreign investor's funds, as described below. No stone can be left unturned if success is the desired result.

This significant increase in EB-5 petitions has created a backlog, and processing times have increased dramatically over the last few years[4]. Applicants are waiting for 18 months and longer (significantly longer for Chinese investors due to retrogression—see footnote below) for a decision on their I-526 conditional green card petitions, and an end to this does not seem to be in sight (although several EB-5 reform proposals address this backlog issues). And, while direct investment EB-5 applications may be subject to somewhat faster processing times, there simply are no guarantees *other than delays!*

---

4. Just before the end of USCIS's fiscal year 2014 (which ended on 9/30/14), the full slate of the 10,000 available EB-5 visas were used for the first time since the program's inception in 1990; however, Chinese immigrant visas began to retrogression in mid-2015, meaning that EB-5 demand for Chinese investor immigrants exceeds the available visas, such that they would need to wait in queue to submit their I-526 petitions, which in mid-2017 meant a 3-year waiting period.

Funding

As noted above, in both direct investment and regional center cases, investors must be able to clearly prove the legal source of their funds. As stated on the USCIS website:

> Any assets acquired directly or indirectly by unlawful means, such as criminal activity, will not be considered capital pursuant to the Immigration and Nationality Act section 203(b)(5) and Title 8 of the Code of Federal Regulations (8 CFR) section 204.6(e). Additionally, per 8 CFR section 204.6(j) and Matter of Ho, 22 I&N Dec. 206 (AAO, 1998), a petition must demonstrate by a preponderance of the evidence that the petitioner's capital was his or her own and was obtained through lawful means.[5]

Whatever the amount ($500,000 or $1 million), wherever the investment is made (which determines the minimum investment) and into which type of entity (direct or indirect) it is invested, the *legitimacy* of the investment capital is *paramount*. The "source of funds" analysis is one of the two critical components of an I-526 petition (see page 154), and the "source" of the funds used for the investment must be traced to the actual source, or as close thereto as possible. For example, if the investor received a gift from his/her parents, the parents' source of the gifted funds must be disclosed.

---

5. U.S. Citizenship and Immigration Services. "EB-5 Interactive Series: Requests for Evidence on Lawful Source of Funds for Investment." USCIS. Accessed March 31, 2017. www.uscis.gov/outreach/notes-previous-engagements/eb-5-interactive-series-requests-evidence-lawful-source-funds-investment.

Notably, the uses of the invested funds must also be demonstrated. This important analysis is known as the "Sources and Uses of Funds," and is usually depicted by a chart included in the business plan, wherein the source of funds might be the investor's capital (and any other capital included) and the uses would represent the ways in which the investor's capital will be utilized within the subject business into which the capital is being invested.

For a direct EB-5 investment, investors can combine cash with equipment, inventory, operations, etc. in order to fulfill the capital investment requirement. Conversely, for an indirect EB-5 investment through a regional center project, investors will most likely be required to come up with actual cash (or cash equivalents) from the outset in order to fulfill the capital investment mandate, since there are no creative ways in which the capital will be utilized or the investment thereof delayed in whole or in part. And, to reiterate, the minimum investment amount is $1 million *unless* the investment is being made into a business or EB-5 project that is located in a TEA, whereupon the minimum investment threshold is reduced to $500,000.

Filing the I-526 Immigrant Investor Petition

For investors, once the subject investment has been chosen and the funds are deposited into escrow (or directly in the case of a direct investment), an I-526 petition (Immigrant Petition by Alien Entrepreneur) is filed with the counsel of an experienced immigration attorney. At the time of this writing, the filing fee for an I-526 petition is $3,675; fees change periodically, so it would be prudent to check the fee schedule at www.uscis.gov before filing the petition.

The I-526 petition represents "notice" to USCIS that an EB-5 investor is making the required investment in an EB-5 regional center project or direct investment opportunity, and he/she is seeking permanent residence in correlation to this investment. The petition requires proof that the project is qualified for EB-5 as supported by appropriate legal business documents such as articles of incorporation and other formation documents. The petition also requires proof that the appropriate amount is being invested[6] and that the capital was acquired legally. This can be proven with bank statements, tax returns, securities statements, etc.—the "source of funds" analysis mentioned above.

The I-526 petition also requires a detailed business plan that is compliant with "Matter of Ho" (see page 172) and demonstrates that the subject business will fulfill the ten full-time job creation minimum requirement within the allotted timeframe. This is the most critical piece of the I-526 puzzle. Without a compliant business plan that is comprehensive and credible, the chances of denial increase exponentially. In the case of a direct EB-5 investment, the business plan must include, along with other corporate documents and business plan requirements, the job creation plans and include in-depth job descriptions and a hiring timeline, and must specifically detail the

---

6. $500,000 or $1 million, respectively, depending on whether the underlying investment is in a TEA or not, the former for which a TEA letter will be required.

role that the foreign investor will play in the day-to-day operations of the business. The investor must be willing to prove his/her hands-on intentions, or the chances of further inquiry and/or denial increase. In a regional center case, the business plan is the single-most important catch-all document comprising part of the offering package (see Chapter 9 entitled "Raising EB-5 Capital and Putting Together an EB-5 Project" for further details).

Once the petition has been filed, it can take upwards of 18 months, as outlined above, for USCIS to do one of three things: issue an approval, request additional evidence (RFE), or deny the application. See Figure 8.1, which represents the process that most investors follow in making investment choices and subsequently pursuing permanent residence.

Figure 8.1. EB-5 Investor Procedure

Petition Approval and Conditional Permanent Residence

If the I-526 petition is approved, the foreign investor can file a Form I-485 (Application to Register Permanent Residence or Adjust Status). This enables the investor to receive conditional permanent residence in the United States for two years. Those two years will allow the investor to carry out his/her investment and confirm that it is indeed viable and fulfills the job creation requirements. If the investor is in the United States in another lawful status when his/her I-526 is approved, he/she can file the I-485 adjustment of status. However, because the I-526 petition takes more than a year to be approved, many foreign nationals are unable to stay in the United States in the interim. In such cases, the investor must return to his/her home country and file a DS-260 form with the National Visa Center (visit https://travel.state.gov/content/visas/en/immigrate/nvc/nvc-contact-information.html for further details on the National Visa Center and its role in immigrant visa processing) in order to enter the United States as a conditional permanent resident based on I-526 approval. Processing will require an interview at a consulate or embassy in the foreign national's home country prior to entry.

"Unconditional" Permanent Residence

The final step in the EB-5 process is the removal of the conditions on permanent residence. If, after two years, the EB-5 investment can be shown to have resulted in the fulfillment of the requirements of the program (monetary investment correlating to the creation of at least ten full-time jobs during the two-year conditional period), the investor is eligible to file a Form I-829 (Petition by Entrepreneur to Remove Conditions on Permanent Resident Status) and, upon approval, to become an *unconditional* permanent resident, along with his/her immediate family members. At the time of this writing, this petition carries an additional filing fee of $3,750; fees change periodically, so it would be prudent to check the fee schedule at www.uscis.gov before filing the petition.

Direct versus Indirect Investment

Since the EB-5 Regional Center Program was established in 1992, the perception has been that the best and easiest route for a foreign investor to take is by way of the passive, indirect regional center investment. There is no day-to-day involvement or participation in the subject business/project required, and the job creation requirements are much more flexible (direct as well as indirect/induced jobs may be included in the job creation projections). However, as with most things, low risk translates to low return, that is, regional center investments often carry very nominal projected returns—the real return on investment in such cases is the coveted green card. Thus, the often daunting direct investment path can become more attractive once a few key points are brought to light.

For the foreign businessperson or entrepreneur seeking to play an active role in building his/her American Dream, the direct investment option provides an opportunity to establish a viable, potentially profitable business in the United States and reap the rewards of what at first appears to be a seemingly riskier option. The capital requirement can be achieved with not just cash, but inventory, equipment, research and development, and other valuable assets joined together. Furthermore, as is the case in a regional center investment, if the subject business is located in a TEA then the capital requirement is substantially lower—location, location, location. One common EB-5 misconception is that the investment amount is determined by whether the investment is made via a regional center versus as a direct investment. However, this is not the case. Instead, the *single* determinant of the minimum required investment is whether or not the EB-5 project/subject business is located in a TEA.

One reason for the confusion is that most regional center projects are located within TEAs, thereby requiring a $500,000 investment (per applicant, as of the date of posting). However, the fact that the investment occurs through a regional center is *not* the determinant of the minimum investment amount. Rather, it is the *location* of the project. Indeed, a regional center project located in a non-TEA would still necessitate a $1 million minimum investment amount. Similarly, however, a direct-investment project can easily be located in a TEA thereby requiring a minimum investment of $500,000. If a direct-investment project is not located in a TEA, the required minimum investment amount is $1 million.

The job creation requirement, frequently the biggest obstacle, should be viewed through a practical lens. The ten full-time jobs can be created over the course of the two years of the investor's conditional permanent residence; the jobs need not all be created at the outset. Further, not all jobs need to be high-level specialty occupations, or for that matter any specific position at all. The jobs can be administrative jobs, sales jobs - even minimum-wage jobs. The key is that they must simply be permanent and full-time (at least thirty-five hours per week) for U.S. workers. Accordingly, it would be prudent for a potential EB-5 investor to seriously consider the direct option.

Direct investment options are endless. The investor is free to invest in any viable business that is likely to be successful and will support the creation of at least ten full-time jobs. The author considers many franchise opportunities to be very viable for direct investment candidates, and they offer many advantages. For example, a franchise offers a turnkey business whereby all of the procedures and systems are set out for the franchisee. This renders many franchises to be tailor-made for the direct EB-5 investor. Few foreign nationals are fully cognizant of the full scope of what it takes to operate a business—particularly a successful business—in the United States. To some degree, a franchise addresses these shortcomings by providing the foreign investor with all of the tools that he/she needs to achieve success, both in terms of running the business and eventually having the green card's initial conditions removed. Business and franchise brokers can be of significant assistance in guiding investors in choosing appropriate franchise opportunities to meet the investor's specific profile, particularly those with a focus on foreign nationals and business visas. However, the fact remains that some investors would prefer to get a green card which does not require their direct involvement, that is, a passive investment in a USCIS-designated regional center project. This path to the American Dream through permanent residence should by no means be discouraged. It is an option that still stimulates the economy and creates jobs for U.S. workers, albeit indirectly.

REAL-LIFE EB-5 SCENARIOS

Scenario 1

Mr. C has been a successful restaurant owner in China for the past fifteen years, but would like to move to the United States to give his two young children access to better education and opportunities. He has been saving vigorously since he opened his first restaurant in China, and after a recent vacation to the southwestern United States, he believes that there is a need for a good, authentic Chinese restaurant in the rural town of Nogales, Arizona, which sits adjacent to the Mexican border and sees approximately $18 billion in cross-border trade annually.

During his vacation, Mr. C happened upon what he believed to be the perfect location for his new restaurant and set things in motion. He met with multiple immigration companies and law firms, both in Arizona and nationwide, and, after retaining the only full-service firm with which he consulted to assist with the many components of his EB-5 visa application, purchased a rundown, closed restaurant building for $150,000.

Upon returning to China, Mr. C set about getting his finances in order, while back in the United States, his attorney hires a team comprised of professional business plan writers and CPAs to put together the required documentation needed for Mr. C's I-526 petition. Mr. C's strong team of hired professionals submits the convincing package to USCIS for review. Upon approval, Mr. C and his family are given a conditional visa, which allows them to reside and work in the United States.

Mr. C sells his restaurant business in China and the family immigrates to Arizona, where Mr. C invests another $350,000 in renovations, new equipment, and hiring a large staff of seventeen full-time employees, as well as some additional part-time workers. The process moves fairly quickly, and in three months, Mr. C's restaurant is open for business. Twenty-three months after approval of Mr. C's I-526 petition, Mr. C's restaurant is booming with business, and his attorney submits an I-829 petition, which, upon approval by USCIS, grants him a permanent green card.

Scenario 2

Ms. M attends a real estate development conference where she is introduced to the EB-5 program for the first time by one of the event's speakers. Ms. M owns a real estate development firm in Chicago, which is currently working on a mixed-use residential project not far from the heart of downtown Chicago. The company expects to be ready to break ground in about five to six months' time, and the total project costs are anticipated to be $100 million. Ms. M's firm originally intended to invest

$15 million in owner equity into the project and then take out an $85 million construction loan to cover the balance of the development costs, but Ms. M is intrigued by the prospect of raising funds through the EB-5 Regional Center Program, since the loan comes with less risk and lower interest costs.

Ms. M exchanges her information with the speaker, who happens to be an immigration attorney and EB-5 expert. The two discuss the project briefly over lunch and the EB-5 expert recommends that if the project is located in a Targeted Employment Area (TEA), Ms. M may be able to raise up to 40 percent in alternative funding from EB-5 investors to offset the construction loan. The EB-5 expert consults with her colleague and confirms that the location is in a TEA, after which Ms. M hires the EB-5 expert and her professional team to assist Ms. M's firm in developing the project and finding an appropriate regional center with which to affiliate the project in order to include the construction jobs in the job creation projections, with the goal of raising $35 million in EB-5 capital, which translates to 70 EB-5 investors and a minimum of 700 jobs created plus a 20 percent job creation cushion, equaling 840 jobs minimum.

Because Ms. M's firm intends to continue to raise funds for future projects through the EB-5 Program, she also decides to proceed with establishing her own regional center, as there are many other projects in the pipeline and this makes more sense than renting a regional center time after time; however, Ms. M, at the urging of the EB-5 expert, decides to table this undertaking until after the project documents have been completed and the project undertakes the process of finding its initial EB-5 investors through broker-dealers and other investment advisors and qualified agents.

Ms. M provides her hired team of EB-5 professionals with the information and documentation necessary to create the package of offering documents compliant with the requirements for the EB-5 Regional Center Program. The team develops an EB-5 business plan, market study, and economic impact report and coordinates with securities and immigration counsel to develop the Private Placement Memorandum (offering document) and Investor Template (I-526 template) for the project, all of which are designed in compliance with USCIS's standards. Notably, the project is projected to create almost a combined 3,000 direct and indirect jobs, which translates to more than thirty jobs per investor. Working together with the EB-5 expert, Ms. M then retains a team of migration brokers and agents to legally seek interested foreign investors to bring to the table at $500,000 apiece (as of the current writing).

Development begins on the project using the owner equity and smaller construction loan, as the EB-5 funds are not *needed* to move forward with the project. Investors come to the table willingly, as the project is well supported and capitalized, and the job creation numbers reflect more than thirty jobs per investor, well in excess of the minimum of ten jobs per investor. Once the project is fully capitalized, including capital from the full slate of seventy EB-5 investors, Ms. M and the EB-5 expert team turn their attention to the creation of the regional center. The EB-5 investors' immigration attorneys file their I-829 petitions in a timely manner as the project's development is completed and the jobs have been created.

Scenario 3

Mrs. S, an American citizen, wants to open up six new pre-schools in San Francisco, California, focused on teaching children both Spanish and English. Mrs. S is projecting approximately $10 million in total setup costs, and antic-ipates that ten to twelve direct, full-time employees will be needed to run each preschool location. Mrs. S has $2 million available to open the first two preschools, but is short $1 million.

Mrs. S's close friend from her days studying abroad in Germany, Ms. G, is interested in investing an additional $500,000 into each of the six new preschools for a total investment of $3 million and 33 percent company ownership. Mrs. S retains an immigration attorney and a team of EB-5 experts to put together an EB-5 compli-ant comprehensive business plan and market study to support the job creation projections to submit to USCIS along with Ms. G's I-526 petition.

After making the initial investment of $1 million into the establishment of the first two preschools, USCIS grants Ms. G conditional permanent residence. Twenty-two months later, the immigration attorney files an I-829 with USCIS on Ms. G's behalf, and upon verification that the business is doing well and more than ten full-time positions have been created, correlating to the initial $1 million investment, USCIS grants approval to remove the conditions from Ms. G's status and her green card becomes permanent.

CHAPTER 9

Raising EB-5 Capital and Putting Together an EB-5 Project: The (Complicated World of) Offering Documents

"You can dream, create, design and build the most wonderful place in the world. But it requires people to make the dream a reality."

—WALT DISNEY

Navigating the EB-5 waters is challenging and time-consuming. However, assembling the right team of experts—including attorneys, analysts, researchers, economists, and business plan designers—can make all the difference in the navigation for regional centers, project developers, business owners, franchisors, and even the investors. EB-5 experts can demystify the complex EB-5 process, paving the path for pain-free EB-5 approval. The right team will leverage its breadth of industry expertise and experience to guide business owners and investors alike in making the right choices to match their needs and goals.

In the often-daunting area of EB-5 and project development, having a single-source point-of-contact to "quarterback" the entire EB-5 process is essential. A quarterback plays the vital role of overseeing all project components, including Matter of Ho–compliant business plans, market feasibility studies, appraisals, economic impact reports, and the multitude of required legal agreements and documentation as well as the filing process, and even fundraising coordination and oversight.

The quarterback should have strong relationships with the parties that are essential to the overall success of the EB-5 process and should work with qualified strategic partners such as economists, marketing experts, licensed EB-5 broker-dealers, migration agents (these are the parties that actually find investors/capital for the projects), immigration and securities attorneys, financial institutions, escrow administrators, and others. These professionals *must* be well-vetted and immediately available to work on new projects. The quarterback must hold these service providers accountable and to strict deadlines and high-quality standards throughout the process, making sure that everything is delivered on *time,* on *budget,* and on *target.* Consistency must be ensured among all documents to ensure a smooth path to approval.

With these strategic partnerships in place, the quarterback provides the full spectrum of services needed for EB-5 approval, throughout the lifecycle of the process from conception of the project or business through its inception and fruition—in other words, from inception to conception and through birth. Working with an experienced quarterback minimizes the need to procure outside services from unrelated sources, which signifi-cantly streamlines the otherwise overwhelming process.

Initial EB-5 Project Assessment

For EB-5 project concepts, the quarterback will first undertake a comprehensive assessment of the proposed project to ensure that it is likely to be successful for EB-5 purposes. This assessment will include an analysis of the following: 1) whether or not the project is in a TEA; 2) the anticipated overall job creation numbers (utilizing the services of an economist), 3) the planned capital stack (the different sources of capital that will comprise the funding for the project, of which EB-5 is one component), 4) an analysis of the market for the business including a competitive analysis, and 5) the anticipated marketabil-ity to prospective investors, utilizing the expertise of an industry broker-dealer, and the financial projections. A preliminary assessment report should be delivered, out-lining any recommended changes that should be made before proceeding with the preparation of the EB-5 project package.

Specifically, before a prospective project sponsor pursues EB-5 funding, it is recommended that he/she retain the services of an experienced EB-5 team to fully vet the project, which vetting should include but not be limited to the following (as applicable):

- **Project readiness/due diligence assessment:** Due diligence services evaluate the viability and feasibility of the project and the likelihood that it will pass the scrutiny of USCIS. The assessment reports should analyze all aspects of the business venture relevant to the EB-5 process, including job creation, marketability, market feasibility (see the next bullet), the geographic location (to determine if it will be located in a TEA), management team analysis, capital stack consideration, and financial review. Confirmation that the proposed project is in a TEA will also be essential.

- **Market feasibility study:** This is an essential component of a thorough due diligence assessment and certainty of any EB-5 project that is used to substantiate the viability of a new business, given then-current conditions and trends, and is critical to the overriding credibility factor for EB-5 business plans.

- **Initial jobs analysis:** The number of jobs a project can create dictates the amount of EB-5 capital that can be raised. Thus, a qualified economist should conduct an initial "job count" using USCIS-approved input/output models to demonstrate the creation of at least ten qualifying jobs per investor.

- **Capital stack analysis:** This involves helping clients determine what proportion of the capital stack can (as opposed to should) come from EB-5 financing and how many EB-5 investors will be needed.

- **Marketability analysis:** This is a critical analysis that must be undertaken before any prospective project sponsor proceeds with the preparation of the EB-5 package as it will provide a snapshot of the likelihood of success in the current competitive EB-5 landscape. Without a high likelihood of success, it is generally not recommended to proceed unless adjustments are made, if appropriate.

- **Legal documentation filing:** Immigration attorneys prepare and file application(s) with USCIS.

Figure 9.1 (below) is a flowchart of the processes and procedures utilized for all stages of the EB-5 project's lifeline—from conception through inception and fundraising. You can use this figure as a reference guide when considering any EB-5 project.

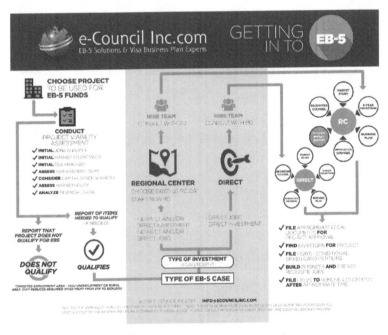

Figure 9.1. Processes and Procedures
for EB-5 Project Lifeline Stages

Once the project has been qualified and any recommended changes are made, the quarterback will enlist experienced EB-5 professionals to perform the following services:

- **Securities counsel:** to create a private placement memorandum and supporting corporate and related documents including loan, subscription, and related agreements, etc. that show, among other things, the relationships between the participating entities.

- **Immigration counsel:** to prepare and file applicable USCIS petition documentation together with all supporting EB-5 package documents.

- **Market study/feasibility study/appraisal:** a comprehensive analysis of the market for the business, including a detailed, location-specific competitive analysis, target market study, and feasibility assessment.

- **Economic impact report (EIR):** a comprehensive report prepared by a qualified economist with specific EB-5 experience using various data sets and formulas to project the number of direct and indirect/induced jobs that the project is likely to create. TEA letters will usually also be ordered by the economist. Note that although an EIR is not required for direct investment cases, TEA letters are required for *all* cases relying on the lower investment threshold.

- **Five-year financial projections:** as calculated or reviewed by a certified public accountant (CPA) experienced with EB-5 requirements.

FINDING YOUR SILVER LINING

- **Matter of Ho-compliant business plans:** It is essential to work with experienced professionals that understand how to build a comprehensive and credible EB-5 business plan that complies with the pivotal 1998 AAO case commonly known as "Matter of Ho." According to this case, there are nine key components in a Matter of Ho-compliant business plan: 1) description of the business, 2) discussion of the business structure, 3) marketing plan with target market analysis, 4) competitive analysis, 5) personnel experience, 6) required licenses and permits, 7) staff timetable for hiring, 8) job descriptions, and 9) budget and financial projections. Not all of these elements must exist in every business plan—for example, in a business plan for a regional center project, job descriptions and a hiring timeline would be virtually impossible for all indirect/induced jobs—but the overall document should satisfy the scope and intention of the requirements.

- **Financial Institutions, Agents, and Other Stakeholders**

In today's competitive EB-5 environment, working with an experienced quarterback can have a significant impact in terms of helping issuers better streamline the otherwise complex EB-5 process and can make the difference between a successful versus an unsuccessful project offering package, which could translate to whether or not the developer/business owner is able to raise EB-5 capital for the subject project.

Regional Center Requirements

Regional centers are government-designated economic entities that are formed to raise EB-5 investment capital for large commercial projects. To receive this government designation and have permission to legitimately accept EB-5 investor capital, these entities must fulfill certain USCIS requirements. These requirements exist to ensure the proposed regional center is fulfilling the original purpose of the EB-5 Immigrant Investor Program—that is, the regional center must have a positive economic impact that is beneficial to the United States and creates jobs for U.S. workers. The regional center applicant must show clearly what the economic benefits are or are expected to be, the total projected cost(s) of the project, how it will positively impact the geographical area it will cover, as well as how it will be operated and by whom.

USCIS requires the filing of Form I-924 (Application For Regional Center Under the Immigrant Investor Program) and, with it, supporting documentation about the proposed project(s) addressing the above requirements. On December 23, 2016, the fee to file this application rose significantly from $6,230 to $17,795. This does not include the cost of producing the documentation required to support the application, including payments to the professional team members.

The proposed regional center project(s) can be in various stages of readiness—they can even be *hypothetical*—that is, they can be full of generalities that are compelling enough to predict their economic benefit; it is even possible to submit documentation for a project that may not ever actually be pursued. As a result, many regional center applications are submitted using hypothetical projects initially in an effort to expedite the processing thereof, while concurrently the actual project may be submitted utilizing an affiliation agreement with an existing regional center while the I-924 is pending.[1] The main advantages of filing an I-924 using a hypothetical project are mainly reflected in the cost and time savings, since both the document preparation period and USCIS's review and designation process will be expedited and significantly less expensive.

If an I-924 is submitted using an *actual* project, it must be backed up with a comprehensive, Matter of Ho–compliant business plan that details the project, offers sound market analysis, includes reasonable financial projections and budgets, and can elaborate on the specifics of job creation and corporate structure. Submitting an I-924 with an actual project means that you must proceed with said project and utilize it to solicit and ultimately raise initial EB-5 capital.

An *exemplar* project is a solid project proposal that has an I-526 petition associated with it. This I-526 petition (Immigrant Petition by Alien Entrepreneur), which was discussed briefly in Chapter 8, is the first step taken by the foreign investor with USCIS on the path to permanent residence. The business plan that the proposed regional center includes with this petition must be EB-5 comprehensive and Matter of Ho–compliant. Essentially, exemplar projects must be "shovel-ready" and on the

---

1. Once the applicant's regional center is designated, the project sponsors can move the project from the affiliated regional center to the proprietary one without resulting in a *substantive* change.

cusp of breaking ground at the time of submission. One of the advantages of this type of project is that future investor petitions will be given deference by USCIS, which generally translates to expedited processing.

Table 9.1 outlines the varying degrees of readiness and requirements for each type of project.

TABLE 9.1. PROJECT READINESS AND REQUIREMENTS COMPARISON

TYPE OF PROJECT	SIMILARITIES/DIFFERENCES
Hypothetical	• General proposals and predictions may be sufficient to determine that the proposed regional center will more likely than not promote economic growth.
	• The business plan *need not* comply with Matter of Ho, although following the guidelines of Matter of Ho is strongly recommended and will pave the way to easier approval once the project becomes actual or exemplar in nature.
	• I-924 decisions are *not* given deference in subsequent filings.
	• Changes can be made to the business plan before the I-526 petition.
Actual	• Verifiable details are required to be supported by economically or statistically sound forecasting tools.
	• A Matter of Ho–compliant business plan is required.
	• I-924 decisions are given deference in subsequent filings.
	• Small changes can be made to the business plan before I-526 petition.

Exemplar

- A significant volume of verifiable detail is required.

- A Matter of Ho-compliant business plan is required.

- A degree of USCIS preapproval will be given to a successful application (deference to future investor petitions).

- Changes cannot be made to the business plan after submission without filing for an amendment.

Once a regional center is designated by USCIS, it must prove its continued compliance annually, specifically in terms of compliance with job creation requirements, or it will risk losing their regional center designation. This would be devastating to the business project and investors alike. Notably, on March 20, 2017, USCIS announced that it would be commencing regional center compliance audits, something that had been a looming promise in the industry for quite some time prior to said date. The goal of these audits is to enhance the integrity of the EB-5 program while ensuring that regional centers continue to meet the goals of the EB-5 program.

Regional Center Job Creation Requirements

As discussed, the direct investment route requires the direct creation or preservation (in the case of a troubled business) of ten full-time jobs. The regional center job creation requirement still exists, but is somewhat more flexible. In addition to direct full-time jobs (at least thirty-five hours per week), indirect and induced job creation can fulfill the regional center mandate.

Indirect jobs could be jobs created by the vendors that supply goods or services to the EB-5 project. Their increased business with the large project means they have to hire more workers. Induced jobs would be the jobs created by workers spending money in the community. The combination of both indirect/induced and direct jobs enables regional center projects to seek significantly more funding from foreign investors because the job creation figures enable significantly greater capital raises. While the jobs must still be created within two years of the initial filing of the I-526, because regional center project investors are staggered in terms of the timing of their investments, the project's job creation is generally considered over a two and a half year period.

Importantly, all of the jobs created and capital spent translates to economic stimulation in the geographic region where the regional center is located. Regional center projects are often huge, such as the building of hotels and infrastructure projects, raising multiple millions of dollars from EB-5, as well as other capital stack sources. Projects on this scale will stimulate any economy in which they operate because of their sheer scale, as well as a variety of other positive factors that enhance their appeal.

Renting an Existing versus Creating a New Regional Center

As discussed, the process of creating a USCIS-approved regional center is complex, expensive, and time-consuming. USCIS approval is never guaranteed. For some U.S. entrepreneurs, renting an established regional center is a viable and attractive option. For some regional center owners, partnering with outside entrepreneurs is appealing if they are having trouble attracting enough EB-5 foreign investors or would like to assume more projects in additional industry designations for which they are approved.

As with any financial transaction, due diligence is required. If the transaction is handled professionally and with the advice of counsel, it is a win-win for all involved. If not, it can be a disaster. The regional center owners can either accept a fixed fee from the outside entrepreneur or negotiate a percentage of the proposed project profits. Either option means more commercial enterprise, more job creation, and economic growth.

REGIONAL CENTER REQUIREMENTS INFOGRAPHIC

REGIONAL CENTER REQUIREMENTS

To qualify for Regional Center designation, it must be shown that the applicant will have a positive economic impact on the U.S. and will create jobs for U.S. workers.

The Regional Center applicant must clearly detail the projected economic benefits, the total cost of the proposed project(s), how it will positively impact the geographical area it will cover and how it will operate.

USCIS requires the filing of an I-924, Application For Regional Center Under the Immigrant Investor Program together with supporting documentation regarding the proposed project(s) addressing the above requirements.

The EB-5 business plan the proposed Regional Center includes with the I-924 petition must be comprehensive, credible and Matter of Ho-compliant.

Once a Regional Center is designated by USCIS, it must prove its continued compliance yearly, specifically in terms of ongoing job creation requirements.

EB-5 PROJECT FAQS

Q: What are the benefits to developers using the EB-5 Regional Center program?

A: The benefits of using the EB-5 Regional Center program include: 1) they offer opportunities to developers seeking alternative funding with minimal risk and a low return on investment (ROI), 2) the funding is available on a non-recourse basis (since the investor's capital must be "at risk", and 3) the funding is generally available by way of a loan model such that the developer need not offer equity to the investors. Through the EB-5 Regional Center program, U.S. business owners and developers can raise capital for large-scale development projects such as hotels, assisted living facilities, and mixed-use projects, as well as smaller-scale projects requiring but a few investors, by applying through USCIS for the ability to raise EB-5 funding. Once a project has been approved by USCIS, foreign investors can make a passive—or in some cases direct—investment of a minimum of $500,000 or $1 million (depending on whether or not the project is located in a TEA) to correlate to the creation of at least ten full-time jobs. Upon making this investment, provided that their I-526 petition is approved, investors will be granted a conditional visa. After two years and as long as the project has not gone belly up, the immigrant investor can apply to have the conditions on his/her visa removed and can begin the transition to a permanent green card and eventually citizenship.

Q: What is the difference between the EB-5 Regional Center Program and the EB-5 Direct Program?

A: The major difference between the two is the types of jobs that can be counted toward each investment made by a foreign investor. With the Direct Program, the only job creation that can be counted toward the project are *direct* jobs—full-time positions directly employed by the project after completion. For example, say you are trying to open a restaurant and wish to seek EB-5 funding. The only jobs you can count toward each investment made by a foreign investor are the full-time employees, employed after the restaurant is open for business—managers, kitchen staff, wait staff, bartenders, etc. This program is typically used for smaller projects, like restaurants, wellness centers, franchises, schools, etc.

Although less complex than the indirect program, business owners are somewhat limited in the amount of capital they can raise through the EB-5 Direct investment Program as there is less flexibility in terms of the job creation numbers. The indirect (regional center) program projects are generally more complicated than direct investment options, but the former provides business owners with the possibility of raising significantly more capital through the EB-5 program by allowing for the inclusion of *indirect* and/or *induced* jobs created by the project. This means that on top of each new full-time position the project intends to create, project sponsors can also include new jobs indirectly created by the project, such as construction jobs. In order to count the indirect jobs created by the project, developers and investors must use a regional center as a middleman.

Q: What is a Regional Center?

A: An EB-5 regional center is an organization designated by USCIS that sponsors capital investment projects for investment by EB-5 investors. In other words, if a project intends to include indirect and/or induced jobs in the job projection estimates, and to raise significantly more funds through the EB-5 program, then the project must either rent or create its own regional center. If you have multiple development projects that potentially qualify for EB-5 funding, then it may be in your best interest to create your own regional center to avoid paying a third-party to oversee the process.

Q: How much will developing an EB-5 Regional Center project cost?

A: This question is difficult to answer. If you are the project developer, the cost can be anywhere from $100,000 to $150,000 for the legal fees and the cost of putting together all the offering documents. The expenditure will vary depending on whether you intend to create your own regional center or rent one.

Q: Are there any Advantages to Raising Capital Through Direct Investment?

A: The EB-5 direct investment option is advantageous for smaller projects seeking to raise less capital and not needing to depend on indirect and/or induced jobs to support the EB-5 capital being sought, as the program is less complex and expensive then its regional center counterpart—for example, an Economic Impact Report is *not* required.

Recent Developments

In recent years, the EB-5 Regional Center Program has become the subject of contentious debate among politicians, developers, and other EB-5 stakeholders. The last-minute, short-term extensions of 2015 and 2016 reflect Congress's inability to agree on meaningful reforms to the program. In December 2016, on the eve of one of many short-term extensions of the EB-5 program and with an inauguration looming on the horizon, Congress passed a continuing resolution extending the EB-5 Regional Center Program through April 28, 2017. On May 1, the Program extension was punted without change through September 30, 2017, by which time bipartisan reform is certainly expected.

Prior to the most recent short-term extensions, the "pilot" program had been extended until September 30, 2015, at which time it was extended for one year until September 30, 2016. Behind-the-scenes efforts continue between EB-5 industry leaders and the House of Representatives Judiciary Committee chairman and ranking members of the Judiciary Committee to reform the program. Despite numerous reauthorization and similar bills presented to the House, by the time of this writing, no resolution had been reached; however, a bipartisan resolution is finally anticipated in the very near future well in advance of the September 30, 2017 deadline.

At the time of this writing, President Trump's specific position on EB-5 remains uncertain, but all indications are positive that he is supportive of the program in general. Trump's significant background in real estate development—an industry that has, in general, benefitted greatly from investment through the EB-5 program—coupled with the fact that he remains "tax averse," indicates greater support for the sometimes-controversial program.

The EB-5 program is undeniably a boon to economic development, utilizing foreign investment dollars as opposed to U.S. taxpayer money to accomplish developmental goals. Additionally, the program's focus is on creating U.S. jobs, something that Trump consistently advocated during the election process and continues to ardently advocate as president. The general feeling in the EB-5 industry and the immigration community is that Trump will, in fact, support and continue the EB-5 program. What remains uncertain is how the program will look in the foreseeable future.

Most pundits believe that the minimum investment amounts will increase in both TEA and non-TEA locations, that the definition of what qualifies as a TEA will be restricted significantly, and that the industry as a whole will see an increased "watchdog" role played by USCIS and other agencies, such as the U.S. Securities and Exchange Commission (SEC), in an effort to minimize the fraud and other issues that have developed over time in the program and have certainly borne a negative impact on its overall perception.

Even most critics of the program believe that the EB-5 Regional Center Program shows great promise in reducing unemployment and revitalizing distressed areas. Rather than do away with it, they want to reform and strengthen it, so misuse is less likely. Indeed, both EB-5 supporters and critics want to leverage the reauthorization process to strengthen the program and fix existing issues. Overall, there is no doubt that a fair review of the whole EB-5 process must acknowledge that it is complex, costly, and time-consuming. In addition, without the assistance of an experienced professional team and proper counsel throughout the complex process, the chances of success in terms of either raising capital or obtaining an EB-5 Immigrant Investor visa decrease drastically.

CHAPTER 10

EB-5–Making a Choice: Direct vs. Indirect (Regional Center) Investment Options

"We are a nation of immigrants. We are the children and grandchildren and great-grandchildren of the ones who wanted a better life, the driven ones, the ones who woke up at night hearing that voice telling them that life in that place called America could be better."

—MITT ROMNEY

As discussed previously, there are two distinct EB-5 paths. The first path is direct investment, which involves an active investment in a business in which the investor will maintain an ongoing role (although that role could be nominal). All jobs must be direct and employees must be employed by the new commercial enterprise (NCE, an ongoing for-profit U.S. company formed after November 29, 1990, into which the EB-5 investment is made). The second path is an indirect or regional center investment, which involves a passive investment in a project that has developed an EB-5 package and offering documents rendering it available to prospective investors. In the regional center option, jobs may be created directly or through indirect/induced means by the NCE or some of its contractors and/or subcontractors, such that construction and related jobs can be included in the job count as determined by formulas utilized in an Economic Impact Report.

Table 10.1 outlines some of the differences between direct and indirect EB-5 investments.

TABLE 10.1. DIRECT INVESTMENT VERSUS INDIRECT INVESTMENT

DIRECT INVESTMENT	REGIONAL CENTER (INDIRECT)
Investor actually wants to start and/or manage a business.	Investor is not interested in starting or running a business.
Business will be creating sufficient direct employment from the outset that will count toward EB-5 job creation.	The only way to satisfy the job creation requirement is to include direct and indirect/induced jobs.
Investor wants to come to live and work in the U.S. to make investment.	Investor wants to spend a significant amount of his or her time outside of the U.S.
Investor wants to have control over business or investment.	Investor is indifferent about controlling the business or investment.
Investor wants to maximize profits from investment.	Investor is less focused on Return on Investment.
Investor has interest in Return on Investment although IMMIGRATION remains priority.	Immigration–rather than investment return–is the real driving force behind investment.

Choosing Wisely

The first step toward permanent residence through the EB-5 visa program is choosing the right commercial enterprise into which to invest and to decide whether the preference is for an active or passive investment. As discussed, investors have a choice between investing in a for-profit viable business they will run on their own or with just a few partners (direct investment), or pooling their money with a large group of investors and entrepreneurs through a USCIS-certified regional center (indirect investment) project.

Commercial enterprises eligible for EB-5 investment run the gamut of industries. For either type of investment, any legal for-profit business is eligible; however, the job creation requirement—that is, the creation of ten full-time jobs *per investor*—must be strictly honored in both cases. Assessing whether the business/project/enterprise will likely successfully fulfill the job creation within the allotted time requirement is critical to the anticipated success of the EB-5 application; that is, there must be adequate evidence to support the contention that the jobs will be created within two years from the date of filing of the initial I-526 for each investor, which generally translates to a two and a half–year job creation period for indirect investment projects, since not all investors file their I-526 petitions at the same time.

In an indirect investment model—that is, a regional center project—both direct and indirect/induced jobs can be included in the job creation numbers of the subject business into which the capital will be invested, whereas in EB-5 direct investment cases, *only direct,* W-2 jobs can be counted. Potential EB-5 investors should study their options carefully and seek the advice of a qualified investment professional and immigration attorney to charter the best course to permanent residence through this program.

Why Choose the Direct Investment Route?

Although the great majority of investments in the EB-5 program continue to be made through regional center projects, an increasing number of investors are interested in participating in a direct investment opportunity. These investors realize that a "hands-on" investment may prove more rewarding and give them more control, since in many cases the investor will have oversight of the day-to day-operations of the commercial enterprise. The direct investor actually has an interest in seeing his/her investment grow and prefers to exercise greater control over the investment than in the "passive" EB-5 regional center investor. With more focus on return on investment (ROI), the direct investor not only gets a green card but also has the opportunity to grow a business and truly become an integral part of the American economy.

In recent years larger, "pooled" direct investment projects have become popular. In these projects, multiple investors may "pool" investment resources into a single direct project, which may involve multiple restaurant or franchise locations, for example. All jobs must still be created directly, even if at multiple locations. There are no specific ownership percentage requirements for EB-5 purposes, however, since multiple investors are involved, an offering package (Private Placement Memorandum and other supporting corporate offering documents) are required.

When and Why Is a Regional Center Option Preferable?

While the EB-5 direct investment requires a minimum investment of $1 million (or $500,000 if in a TEA) as well as the direct creation or preservation of ten full-time jobs, the EB-5 regional center investment requires $500,000 in a TEA and the direct, indirect, or induced creation of ten full-time jobs. Not having to directly create or preserve ten full-time jobs gives the investor greater flexibility. When the EB-5 Regional Center Program was created in 1992, the hope was that this expansion of the job creation requirement would mitigate the burden of direct job creation.

The EB-5 Regional Center Program has taken off in the last decade, in part because traditional lending routes have become difficult and burdensome. New and creative ways of funding projects are required when the economy is weak and banks don't want to lend money. By forming a regional center, developers and entrepreneurs can create a win-win scenario. They can accept foreign investor capital to complete their large business projects and avoid traditional lending, and they can facilitate the legal immigration of qualified foreign nationals.

Another advantage of investing in a regional center project is that the investor's green card, and therefore ability to remain in the United States with his/her family, does not correlate to the success of his/her own business in the United States, but rather correlates to the overall success of a generally larger-scale business that is well-capitalized and supported and therefore better positioned to face and overcome potential challenges or setbacks.

Choosing the Right Regional Center/ Regional Center Project

Choosing the right regional center, or essentially choosing into which regional center project to invest, is critical. Prospective EB-5 foreign investors and their investment advisors and counsel must undertake proper due diligence before making selections. Unfortunately, many regional centers have lost their designations and/or defrauded investors. Projects have failed, and I-526 petitions have been denied, resulting in the foreign investor losing his/her money and not receiving a green card, which was often the primary motivation for investing in the first place. To have the best chance of succeeding in an EB-5 endeavor, the greatest care must be taken in every aspect of the application process. There are no guarantees, but there is due diligence which can greatly improve the likelihood of success.

When reviewing and studying regional centers and their projects, investors must ask themselves some key questions prior to making their investment, including:

- How long has the regional center been so designated by USCIS?

- How many and what type of EB-5 projects, if any, has the regional center completed?

- What percentage of the regional center project(s) is EB-5 funded?

- How much experience do the principals of the regional center have?

- What jobs are being created? Direct, indirect, induced, or a combination? What is the percentage of each?

- How many investors are in the project?

- What geographical area is the regional center serving?

- Is any part of the investment refunded if the I-526 petition is denied?

- What is the regional center projects' expected return on investment (ROI)?

- What is the risk associated with this investment?

- Does the regional center work with experienced immigration and other counsel? What business model does the regional center use? Corporate structure? Financial reporting? Job creation tracking?

- Does the regional center distribute quarterly reports? Annual reports?

- How are the invested funds and transfers between entities tracked?

These are just some of the questions that should be asked prior to committing to making an EB-5 investment through a particular regional center. Since a foreign investor is not required to be in the same area or even the same state as the regional center into which they invest (unlike the direct investment where they must usually be hands-on and therefore in close proximity), they have a choice among the numerous USCIS-designated regional centers, and therefore multitudes of potential green card–facilitating investments since most regional centers represent several EB-5 projects.

Why Choose the Regional Center Investment Route?

For the EB-5 regional center foreign investor, the driving force for the investment is usually the immigration benefit. The regional center investor is not seeking to start or grow a business or to be a hands-on business owner. He/she is not interested in being involved in the day-to-day operations of the business. He/she simply wants to *passively* make the required $500,000 (low risk/low return) investment into a qualified project affiliated with a USCIS-designated regional center and achieve permanent residence for him/herself and his/her immediate family. Regardless of motivation, EB-5 regional centers and the foreign investors that contribute capital to them clearly stimulate the U.S. economy and create jobs. In so doing, the investor is able to fulfill the most critical and beneficial requirements for permanent residence.

WHICH EB-5 ROUTE SHOULD I TAKE?
INFOGRAPHIC

WHICH ROUTE
SHOULD I TAKE?

DIRECT INVESTMENT
It requires a minimum investment of $1MM (or $500K if in a Targeted Employment Area) as well as the direct creation or preservation of ten full-time jobs.

Having a "hands-on" direct investment may prove more rewarding and ultimately less risky since they have oversight of the day-to day-operations of the commercial enterprise.

REGIONAL CENTER
It requires a minimum investment of $1MM (or $500K in a Targeted Employment Area) and the direct, indirect or induced creation of ten full-time jobs. Not having to directly create or preserve ten full-time jobs gives the investor greater flexibility.

By forming a Regional Center, developers and entrepreneurs can create a win-win scenario.

Regional Centers can accept foreign investor capital to complete their large projects, often avoiding traditional lending, while facilitating the legal immigration of qualified foreign nationals.

EB-5 VISA
The EB-5 visa offers two distinct paths:

1. Involves an active investment in a business in which the investor will maintain an ongoing role, all jobs must be direct and employees must be employed by the NCE.

2. Involves a passive investment in a business that has developed an EB-5 package and offering documents rendering it attractive to prospective investors. The investor does not have an ongoing role and job creation may be direct and indirect/induced.

EB-5 INVESTOR FAQS

Q: What is an EB-5 direct investment?

A: An EB-5 direct investment allows immigrant investors to obtain green cards by making an active investment into a new or existing U.S. business. In order to qualify as an EB-5 direct investment, the project must create (or preserve) at least ten full-time *direct* positions—i.e., persons employed full-time to assist in the projects day-to-day operations—for each $500,000 or $1 million (depending on whether or not the project is located in a TEA) investment from a foreign investor. Indirect jobs, such as construction jobs, cannot be included in the job count for an EB-5 direct investment project.

Q: What are the benefits of an EB-5 direct investment?

A: The EB-5 direct investment model helps foster job growth while simultaneously boosting the U.S. economy. Foreign investors and entrepreneurs who immigrate through the EB-5 program have the benefit of starting their own business in the U.S. and using that business as a means to obtain a conditional green card and eventually citizenship.

Q: What is required for a direct EB-5 application?

A: Evidence that at least ten indirect or induced jobs will be created (or preserved) for each investment made by a foreign investor; evidence that the applicant has already invested in, or is actively in the process of investing in, a new commercial enterprise (NCE) or an existing U.S. business; evidence that the foreign capital was obtained by lawful means; and evidence that the NCE has been established and owns 100% of the job creating entity (JCE). If applicable, evidence that the subject business is in a TEA.

Q: How much will my EB-5 direct investment I-526 application cost?
A: Roughly $50,000 for the I-526 legal petition, business plan and market study components of a Direct EB-5 project, plus filing fees. Please note that this is an estimate and will most likely vary depending on the complexity and nature of the project itself.

Q: How long is the Direct EB-5 visa application process?
A: It varies, but typically the process for an EB-5 direct application takes about 12 to 18 months for an applicant to receive a conditional green card, which is valid for two years. Within 90 days of the two-year anniversary of the project's commencement, provided that the requisite jobs have been created, the applicant can then petition USCIS to have the green card's conditions removed.

Q: What is a TEA and how do I know if my project/ investment qualifies?
A: TEA is the acronym for Targeted Area of Employment. A TEA is an area of high unemployment (at least 150% greater than the national average unemployment rate) and/or a rural area. If your project is located in a TEA, then it qualifies for the lower minimum investment requirement of $500,000. By allowing immigrant investors to

make a smaller investment for the same benefits, TEAs encourage economic growth and job creation in areas of need. Typically, foreign investors are more likely to invest in a project located in a TEA due to the lower investment thresholds. To qualify a location as a TEA, it is recommended that an economist's expertise be sought. The economist will consider the actual location as well as the data of the surrounding area (census tracts) and, if the location qualifies, the state in which the project is located will generally be asked to issue a letter to this effect.

Q: How much would it cost to pursue investment via a Regional Center project?

A: As a passive immigrant investor, this would include the minimum of $500,000 (or $1 million if the project is not located in a TEA) for the investment itself, plus an additional administrative fee averaging $50,000 to be paid to the project sponsor or regional center; the USCIS filing fee of at least $1,500 for an I-526 petition; and any legal fees incurred from retaining an immigration attorney to assist with the application process (average $20,000 as of the time of writing).

Q: How long is the I-526 application process for Regional Center investments?

A: It varies, but typically the process for applying through the EB-5 regional center program takes about 15 months to two years for an applicant to receive a conditional green card, which is valid for two years. Upon evidence of the initial success of the business and job creation within the two years following the approval of the I-526, the applicant can then petition USCIS to remove the conditions of the green card.

Q: Can I bring my spouse and/or children?

A: Yes. No matter what investment, the applicant's spouse and/or unmarried children under age 21 are eligible to reside in the United States for the duration of the beneficiary's EB-5 visa.

Q: Are there any travel restrictions on a conditional or permanent green card?

A: No. There are no travel restrictions and visa holders can come and go as they please.

Q: As a foreign investor, what happens if the business into which I invest fails?

A: Unfortunately, this is one major risk of investing in the EB-5 program. Should the business into which you invested fail before the conditions of your permanent residence are removed, your conditional visa will expire, and you leave the United States and potentially start the process over again. Additionally, there are no investment protections set in place, and there is no guarantee that your money will be returned. However, you should not let this deter you; hiring a team of EB-5 professionals to do the due diligence by assessing potential projects and guiding you through the process will significantly decrease the risks associated with EB-5 regional center projects. Additionally, portability of invested capital is one of the hot-ticket items currently being considered in EB-5 reform.

Q: What professionals do I need to hire in order for my direct investment application to be successful?

A: A prospective immigrant investor will need an expert EB-5 immigration attorney to handle the visa application, as well as a team of EB-5 experts who can guide them through the myriad of available projects and help the investor choose; or, if the investor is making a direct investment and/or setting up their own business, he/she will need a compliant and credible business plan supported by a comprehensive market feasibility study (which is needed to augment the business plan's credibility).

REAL-LIFE EB-5 INVESTOR SCENARIOS

Scenario 1

Mr. F currently works in a high-level management position for a large electronic retailer in Brazil. He manages multiple locations and is very comfortable in his position, but his lifelong dream has always been to move to America and open his own business—only he has never been quite sure what exactly that business would look like. Mr. F's parents recently passed away, leaving him enough money to pursue his American dream.

While researching his immigration options online, Mr. F discovered the EB-5 program and all the possibilities it offers. He contacts a couple EB-5 expert immigration firms and consults with a few attorneys, including a full-service EB-5 concierge. The concierge's business broker expert suggests the possibility of investing in a

U.S. franchise. Mr. F loves this idea, as the business will be owned and operated by him, but there is an added level of security and confidence in its likely success, since the franchise systems are pre-set and the business is essentially turnkey.

Mr. F retains the concierge team that recommended pursuing a franchise investment, and the team assists Mr. F to select a suitable U.S. franchise into which to invest based on his unique circumstances, experience and business goals. After careful deliberation, Mr. F decides to apply to the Friendly Fitness franchise, in order to purchase and open a new branch in Philadelphia, Pennsylvania. After interviewing Mr. F and reviewing his personal financials, Friendly Fitness approves Mr. F for ownership and his concierge professional team develops an EB-5 compliant business plan supported by a market study and customized pro forma financials to submit with Mr. F's I-526 petition.

USCIS approves Mr. F's petition, and he quits his job in Brazil, moving to Philadelphia with his conditional green card in hand. In the first thirteen months after Mr. F is admitted to the United States, he invests over $1 million of his inheritance in his franchise buy-in to purchase an old gym and convert it into a new Anytime Fitness, update the facilities and equipment, and hire a total of thirteen full-time employees, as well as some additional part-time staff. Business is booming, and Mr. F retains the same attorney who did his I-526 petition to put together an I-829 petition to remove the conditions of his green card just before the two-year anniversary of his I-526 approval date. After another sixteen months pass, USCIS approves Mr. F's I-829 petition, and he officially becomes a permanent U.S. resident.

Scenario 2

Mr. and Mrs. L are recently retired Italian nationals, who own a small number of investment properties that they rent through a property management company to vacationers in their hometown in Italy. Their only child lives and works in the United States. The couple has always dreamed of relocating to sunny Florida to be near their daughter and grandchildren, but they would also like to continue to enjoy their retirement.

Mrs. L hires an immigration concierge firm based in Florida, and the concierge coordinates the components and consults with an EB-5 investment advisor and hires an immigration attorney to guide them through the immigration process. Together with the EB-5 team, Mr. and Mrs. L decide that making a passive investment through the EB-5 Regional Center program is their best option for getting everything they want—namely, the ability to reside in the United States, and to share the same rights and benefits as all other U.S. permanent residents, all while continuing to enjoy their retirement.

While Mr. and Mrs. L sell their home and their investment properties in Italy, the immigration team conducts appropriate due diligence and works on finding them a suitable EB-5 project into which the couple could invest, which is located in a TEA close to their desired home location in Florida so that they can visit the project from time to time. The investment advisor consults with the attorney and concierge and then recommends a couple of projects to Mr. and Mrs. L upon which the investment advisor has already completed appropriate due diligence, and the couple chooses the one they like best.

Mr. and Mrs. L first apply to invest in the EB-5 project. Once approved, Mr. L has his bank in Italy transfer $550,000 ($500,000 for the TEA investment and an additional $50,000 to cover the regional center's administrative costs), which can clearly be traced from the sale of the couple's properties in Italy, the monies for which were earned through traceable employment income to Mr. and Mrs. L combined to an escrow account managed by the project's designated regional center.

After the investment is placed and accepted in the selected project's escrow account, Mr. and Mrs. L's attorney uses the project's offering documents to prepare and submit the couple's I-526 Immigrant Petition by Alien Entrepreneur (which includes the requisite source of funds analysis to ensure that the money being invested is traceable and derived from a lawful source) with USCIS to secure their conditional green cards.

Once USCIS grants Mr. and Mrs. L said status, the couple moves into their newly purchased retirement condo and begin their lives as American citizens. Additionally, the $500,000 they invested clears the escrow account and is put to use by the project. Shortly thereafter, the couple starts to see a small return on their investment. Two years after Mr. and Mrs. L were first admitted into the United States on a conditional visa, their attorney files an I-829 (Petition by Entrepreneur to Remove Conditions on Permanent Resident Status) to have the conditions removed from the green card, thus adjusting the couple's status to permanent residents. USCIS looks over the petition, verifies that the requisite jobs were created and capital utilized appropriately as set out by the business plan, and approves Mr. and Mrs. L's petition. Mr. and Mrs. L are now full-fledged U.S. green card holders, and can expect to receive a return on investment from the project company until the $500,000 has been paid back in full, plus interest.

CHAPTER 11

The Critical Importance of a Strong Business Plan

"By failing to prepare (plan),
you are preparing (planning) to fail."

—BENJAMIN FRANKLIN,
FOUNDING FATHER OF THE UNITED STATES

A business plan is a roadmap for the development and, ultimately, success of an enterprise. Business plans are an essential element of business visa application packages and must be customized to meet USCIS's specific requirements. There is no doubt that a strong business plan (or the lack thereof) can make (or break) a business visa case. Table 11.1 on the following page highlights a few of the basic differences between traditional versus non-immigrant visa business plans, as their scope and focus are quite distinct.

E-1/E-2 Business Plans

For USCIS to know with some degree of certainty that the non-immigrant visa applicant is a strong candidate for

TABLE 11.1. TRADITIONAL VERSUS VISA BUSINESS PLAN ELEMENTS

Issue	Traditional Business Plans	Visa Business Plans
Business Owner Nationality	Irrelevant	Relevant + for E-1 and E-2 visas, the owner and/or beneficiary must be from treaty signatory country; no specific requirement for L-1 cases
Investment Purposes	Aimed at seeking third-party capital	Capital investment will be required and, for E-2 visas, investment must be "substantial", the determination of which depends on the business type and model
Financial Projections	Focus on ROI	Three- or five-year projections (depending on type of visa) to demonstrate that subject business is likely to grow and sustain more than just owner and family (assumptions are important)–needs to have broader economic impact and employ staff–business must not be MARGINAL
Staffing Plans	The lower, the better	Strong staff numbers demonstrate credibility of business and intention to hire U.S. persons–the higher, the better. Also provides credibility to prove non-marginality in E-2 cases, and to support essential element of manager or executive status in L-1 cases
Office Space	Irrelevant	Adequate space (leased/purchased) to house business and expansion can be critical to visa approval, especially in L-1 cases where virtual office often challenged

approval, the applicant must provide detailed supporting documentation and, specifically, a business plan. Indeed, as of 2006, USCIS *requires* that an applicant's petition for an E-2 visa must include a comprehensive business plan.[1] The regulations' vague language in defining a substantial investment make inclusion of detailed financial projections and a full explanation thereof in the business plan crucial to an application's success.

For both the E-1 and E-2 treaty trader/investor visas, the business plan must denote not only proof of treaty country nationality, but also details about the business dealings to be carried out in the United States, proof of the investment to be made, and projections for business growth and success. The best way to do this is to secure a professional, experienced team to prepare an immigration-specific business plan. This will ensure that this critical document includes competitive analyses, five-year projections, corporate structure, and the many other criteria, all specifically tailored to meet USCIS standards. Through a professionally prepared business plan inclusive of reasonable financial projections, it can be shown that the commercial or entrepreneurial undertaking is "real and operating." Some of the documents necessary to provide evidence that the business is active include leases, licenses, contracts, tax returns, employee tax records, proof of contribution to the U.S. economy, and proof of capital changing hands, rather than sitting in a bank account.

---

1. Immigration Business Plan. "E2 Visa Business Plan Sample—Why Go the E2 Route?" Immigration Business Plan. Accessed April 24, 2017. www.immigrationbusinessplan.com/e2-visa-business-plan-sample.html.

In the case of an E-2 specifically, in addition to the overreaching "substantial investment" and "non-marginality" requirements, many consulates have adopted unique ways of interpreting related E-2 business plan requirements. Table 11.2 below is a comparison of the differing business plan requirements and restrictions of ten sample countries.

TABLE 11.2. COMPARISON OF BUSINESS PLAN REQUIREMENTS

COUNTRY	BUSINESS PLAN REQUIREMENTS
Canada	• Five-year financial projections • Projections must be supported by a complete and thorough business plan
Colombia	• Analysis of the local market and competition • Five-year financial projections • Projections must be backed up by outside sources
France	• Five-year financial projections • The plan must verify the capacity of the enterprise to realize a profit within a maximum of five years
Germany	• A comprehensive plan for the next five years
Israel	• A comprehensive plan for the next five years
Italy	• Evidence that there is present or future capacity to generate more than enough income for a minimal living for the treaty investor and his/her family • The business plan must verify the capacity of the enterprise to realize a profit within a maximum of five years • E visa packages must not exceed forty double-sided pages (including petition)

Japan	• Specific details of the business to be conducted
	• One-, three-, and five-year financial projections for business expenses, sales, gross income and profits or losses
Mexico	• Analysis of the local market and competition
	• Five-year financial projections
	• Projections must be backed up by outside sources
Spain	• Visa application must not exceed fifty pages
United Kingdom	• Comprehensive analysis of the market and competition
	• Five-year financial projections which must be backed up by objective third-party sources

Some U.S. consulates, such as those located in Colombia, Mexico, and the UK, have similar documentation requirements that must be satisfied in order to defeat marginality. However, as Table 11.1 demonstrates, other business plan requirements are vague in terms of the specific evidence requested. Additionally, increasing numbers of consulates are requiring that new businesses be "real and operating" before they will approve the visa. Therefore, if the applicant cannot show that the new business commenced operations prior to the consular interview, the E-2 visa application *may well not be approved.* This makes an all-inclusive, professionally prepared business plan even more essential.

L-1 Business Plans

To secure an L-1A Intracompany Transferee Visa, an applicant must meet specific criteria outlined in the regulations. Employees transferred to the United States to establish a "new office" have the additional burden of proving the potential of the new office to support a high-level executive or managerial employee within one year. The best vehicle to use in satisfying this burden is a comprehensive, professional business plan. For the L-1 intracompany transfers, a business plan is important to prove the petitioning organization is a qualifying organization and the foreign national meets the transfer requirements, either managerial, executive, or specialty knowledge. A properly prepared L-1 business plan will provide convincing evidence of the financial viability of the business transferring the foreign national and will include a detailed organizational structure with job descriptions and financial projections.

Notably, an AAO 2015 appeal case demonstrated to what degree a business plan can *make or break* a case. In this appeal, the petitioner wanted to employ the beneficiary as the president of a new office in the United States pursuant to the guidelines for an L-1A non-immigrant intracompany transferee. The petitioner stated that the employee would be involved in "the overall vision and management of the company's efforts to establish itself as a solid force in the North American market." Despite a lengthy business plan submitted with the petition, USCIS director found the information submitted insufficient to demonstrate that the new company would support a managerial or executive position within one year. Clearly, it is the *quality* of the business plan that is the key to success. Much of what the petitioner failed to provide could have been cured with a professionally written, well-researched, and organized business plan.

Recently, there have been an increasing number of Requests for Evidence (RFEs) in "new office" L-1A cases, most of which have in some significant way fallen short as a result of the contents and/or quality of the business plan. For example, many RFEs have identified vague business plans that failed to provide adequate evidence of appropriate research, competitive analyses, detailed strategies, startup timetables, personnel hiring plans and job descriptions, marketing plan with target dates, and other elements that are akin to those required of EB-5 business plans, as outlined below.

EB-5 Business Plans

For EB-5 visas, the business plan requirement reaches yet another level of complexity and necessity. Because it is a direct route to (initially conditional) permanent residence, the standards are strict and the bar is high. An EB-5 business plan is *the* key document for approval in this category. The overriding consideration is that the business plan must be *credible,* as determined by USCIS, and that all data must be appropriately supported, sourced and cited. It must detail with specificity the job creation and economic impact of the proposed direct investment or regional center project. It must include detailed financial information and market analysis, as well as personnel descriptions, organizational structure, proof of required licenses and permits, and credible growth and success projections.

According to *Matter of Chawathe, 25 I&N Dec. 369, 375–376 (AAO 2010)*[1], the petitioner or applicant must establish each element in question through a *preponderance of the evidence.* The preponderance of the evidence standard dictates that the evidence submitted must show what is claimed is at least 51 percent more likely than not true. As such, not *all* doubt needs to be removed. Thus, even if *some* doubt is left with the adjudicator regarding the verity of the evidence, provided that a substantial volume of credible evidence was submitted to show to demonstrate that the claim is *probably true,* then the standard has been met. The standard of "preponderance of the evidence" is a much lower standard of proof than what is required in a criminal case, wherein the prosecution needs to prove the case beyond a reasonable doubt. If the EB-5 business plan is deemed to not meet the standard then, at best, the application will be returned with a request for further evidence, or at worst, may be denied outright. For a further discussion of the components of a Matter of Ho–compliant business plan, see Chapter 9.

No matter what the evidentiary standard, it is clear that EB-5 business plans are particularly complex and undoubtedly require the expertise of experienced and knowledgeable attorneys, economists, financial planners, and others familiar with EB-5 requirements. Ensuring that the application business plan is complete and thorough from the outset is what gives the EB-5 application the greatest chance for approval. And ultimately it is of paramount importance that the business plan be *credible*—this element is the key distinction between an acceptable business plan and one that fails on its face.

Given that more than a very high percentage of recent denials of administrative appeals of EB-5 petition rejections involve the failure to submit a credible (comprehensive and compliant) business plan, there is no doubt that it is extremely important to provide a competent and comprehensive business plan with the original EB-5 petition. In making sure that a complete and coherent business plan accompanies the petition, petitioners and their counsel will help avoid costly and time-consuming delays and RFEs, as well as other potential hazards.

REAL-LIFE BUSINESS PLAN SCENARIOS

Scenario 1

Mr. U is a Mexican national who wants to invest $500,000 dollars into opening a Mexican restaurant in Boston, Massachusetts, by making a direct investment through the EB-5 Program. He has prior experience in the restaurant business and knows how to write a quality business plan, having prepared many for his prior restaurant endeavors. He has done all the research and crunched the numbers and found he could save quite a bit of cash by filing his I-526 petition on his own instead of hiring a team of professionals. Mr. U writes up a 123-page, incredibly detailed business plan and submits it to USCIS along with the I-526 petition, pays the applicable filing fees, and waits for his approval letter.

Just shy of a year later, Mr. U receives a letter from USCIS, but it is not what he'd hoped for. Instead of approval from USCIS, he receives a Request for Evidence

(RFE), which lists all the missing documentation, such as a TEA letter from the state of Massachusetts or a similar body certifying that the restaurant's location is in fact in a TEA and a market study highlighting the restaurant's potential for success and the details of comparable businesses including job creation, pricing, services, target markets, etc. The RFE further states that the business plan that was submitted is not EB-5 compliant and must be overhauled completely. Additionally, the RFE outlines the requirements to prove the legitimacy of the source of the funds used for the EB-5 restaurant investment.

Unsure how to proceed, Mr. U reaches out to one of the few immigration firms he spoke with during his initial research and retains them to get the petition done correctly. They recommend a professional business plan company to review and transform the business plan so that it is EB-5 complaint, together with a supporting market study and competitive analysis, while simultaneously requesting a TEA letter from the state. The team of professionals oversees the process and turn in the requested evidence and documentation to USCIS once the process is complete.

Sixteen months later, Mr. U receives his approval letter and moves to the United States on his conditional green card to pursue his American Dream. Mr. U maintains an ongoing dialogue with his team of professionals and, shortly before the two-year anniversary of the approval of his I-526 conditional green card, the same professionals handle his I-829 petition, providing proof of the direct job creation set out in the compliant business plan, so that the conditions from his green card can be removed.

Scenario 2

Ms. Z is a Brazilian national who works in an executive-level position for a small Brazilian cosmetics company. The company wants to expand its operations to the U.S. markets and set up an affiliate in California and intend to send Ms. Z to San Diego to establish the new branch office.

The company hires a qualified immigration firm with an in-house business plan team to guide the company and, in particular, Ms. Z through the L-1A immigration process. The immigration firm gathers all the necessary documentation from Ms. Z and the cosmetics company and roughly five weeks later submits an I-129 petition along with an L-1A compliant business plan on Ms. Z's behalf. Wanting to fast-track things, the company spends a little extra on the premium processing fee, and fifteen days later Ms. Z receives USCIS approval of her L-1A visa. Shortly thereafter, she moves to San Diego where she successfully facilitates the expansion of the Brazilian cosmetics company.

CHAPTER 12

Why Hire
a Professional Team?

*"Be a yardstick of quality. Some people aren't used
to an environment where excellence is expected."*

—STEVE JOBS

There are some aspects of American law that can be
understood by laypersons and some legal forms that
can be completed with relative ease without hiring an
attorney. This is risky no matter what, but with immigration law, it is *strongly* discouraged, and *particularly* with
EB-5, whether on the investor or developer side. There
are simply too many moving pieces, and the law is too
complex and layered to even attempt self-representation.

Many of the visas discussed in this guide have some
similarities in process and requirements, but the subtle
variations make all the difference. If anything is overlooked or compromised, it can be fatal to the case. In
many cases, people's lives, in essence, lie in the process.
Only experienced business immigration attorneys and
industry experts truly know how to confirm if all the
boxes are checked when preparing a petition and a

corresponding credible business plan and other supporting documentation. Only these experienced parties can offer the correct advice when deciding which visa is the right one for the specific circumstances of a given case, and only these trusted advisors can properly oversee and coordinate all of the moving parts essential to a successful EB-5 project or investment. The need for professional legal and related help cannot be overemphasized.

As noted, an immigration attorney is not the only professional who is needed to be successful in the business immigration process; there are a multitude of other key team members who play a pivotal role in the success or failure of the subject endeavor, whether from the perspective of the prospective foreign national who is seeking a business visa seeker or the domestic U.S. business seeking to raise significant capital from foreign investors to fund their development or expansion.

A single-source quarterback can provide a level of guidance and oversight that is unparalleled and can save investors and businesses significant time, money, and frustration in the process. This quarterback will utilize his/her strategic relationships to ensure that the best possible team is assembled so that the beneficiary, be it the foreign investor or the U.S. business, can rest easy knowing that they are in good hands.

In business immigration cases, a quarterback serves in a role similar to that of a general contractor in a construction project. The quarterback will help you to cover all of the necessary bases and ensure that what you don't know won't be detrimental to your ultimate success. Having a single-point person who maintains ultimate oversight of the process will help pave the path with as few roadblocks or obstacles as possible, guiding you through and throughout the process with relative ease. You can sleep better at night knowing that the quarterback knows what he/she is doing and has your back.

The quarterback will oversee the selection of the professional team members, each of whom will be tenacious in his/her pursuit of the right solutions customized to satisfy you and your needs. Professional team members will be focused on results, so that you can focus on building the business that is the subject of the immigration case. Collectively, as experts navigating the challenging waters known as U.S. business immigration, the professional team will bridge any gaps in the process.

Choosing to work with a professional team coordinated by a quarterback can make the difference between approval and denial. This team, directed by a quarterback, will demystify the complex process and hold your hand every step of the way.

REAL-LIFE PROFESSIONAL TEAM SCENARIOS

Scenario 1

Mrs. F is an Italian national who wants to open a bed and breakfast in Portland, Oregon. She researches her options online and decides that making a direct investment in a TEA location through the direct EB-5 program is the best path for her to pursue. She immediately retains a U.S. immigration attorney whose firm is not only experienced in EB-5 petitions, but works closely with a full-service concierge EB-5 team prepared to complete the business plan and corresponding market study. Mrs. F wants to hire another company to prepare the supporting documents as the price differential is substantial, but after careful consideration and consultation with the immigration attorney, she is swayed to work with the professional team, confident that her chances of success will increase multifold in so doing.

Once Mrs. F makes her first payment, the team sends her a checklist outlining all of the information and documentation needed to start the process. Mrs. F delivers everything to them in a timely fashion, and about four weeks later, the documents are sent to Mrs. F and the immigration attorney so that the I-526 package can be completed. In the meantime, the attorney handles the source of funds analysis, and once the package is delivered, it is quickly finalized and submitted to USCIS together with the requisite filing fees.

Thirteen months later, Mrs. F's I-526 is approved, and she immigrates to Portland where she gets her business up and running. When the attorney contacts Mrs. F to remind her of the need to get started on the I-829 petition, she is excited to do so and happy that her business is thriving and the twenty-two jobs that have been created are well in excess of the ten job creation minimum. Eighteen months following the filing of the I-829, USCIS grants approval to remove the conditions of Mrs. F's green card, and she looks forward to applying for citizenship after another five years pass.

Scenario 2

Mr. O is a Canadian national who wants to invest his savings ($200,000) into the opening of a dry cleaning business in Detroit. After speaking with a few U.S. immigration attorneys, he concludes that the E-2 visa is the way to go. To save a little money, he retains the cheapest attorney, who assures him that the business plan is not crucial to the petition and that Mr. O can get away without it, thereby saving time and money.

The attorney puts together Mr. O's E-2 petition and schedules his interview with the Toronto consular office. Mr. O attends the interview prepared for a quick approval, only to be asked within minutes of arrival to produce the required business plan. Since he had been advised that a business plan was not needed, Mr. O was unable to produce one and was sent away and told to reschedule once the business plan was ready.

Mr. O immediately fires the original immigration attorney, retains a more qualified and experienced concierge attorney, and decides to restart the application process. This time, however, he is committed to ensuring that everything is done correctly and that no corners are cut in order to save a little money, since his future is at stake, as is the success of his dry cleaning business. His new petition is submitted with the business plan, the interview is scheduled, and his E-2 visa is quickly approved at the time of his attendance.

Mr. O retains the same immigration concierge firm to handle his E-2 renewal five years later, and eventually, when Mr. O is ready to expand his dry cleaning business and invest the additional requisite capital to qualify, as well as adding to the number of positions created within the company, he retains the same immigration concierge to assist with transitioning from an E-2 visa to a green card through the direct EB-5 program. A new business plan is developed to support the EB-5 petition, together with a supporting market study.

Conclusion

"Born in other countries, yet believing you could be happy in this, our laws acknowledge, as they should do, your right to join us in society, conforming, as I doubt not you will do, to our established rules."

—THOMAS JEFFERSON, FOUNDING FATHER
& 3RD PRESIDENT OF THE UNITED STATES

The United States welcomes and indeed encourages the entry of qualified foreign workers, executives, and entrepreneurs, and has created a variety of employment-based immigrant and non-immigrant visas to cater to this demographic. These visa categories, however, come with very specific requirements and, in some cases, limits. As I have discussed in this guide, at times the requirements can seem daunting and the process overwhelming. That is why hiring immigration professionals not only mitigates some of the confusion, but more importantly, raises the chances of approval significantly.

It is strongly recommended to avoid the pain and struggle of going it alone, even with the help of this guide.

Instead, be sure to seek the guidance of qualified legal counsel and other professionals, including business plan professionals, tax and investment experts, and trusted advisors to provide appropriate advice throughout the challenging journey. In all cases, I wish you the best of luck in pursuing your American Dream! We at e-Council, Inc., are here to guide you every step of the way!

SERVICES OFFERED BY E-COUNCIL INC.

Just keep swimming.

—DORY, DISNEY CHARACTER, *FINDING NEMO* (2003)
AND *FINDING DORY* (2016)

At e-Council Inc., we offer turnkey business immigration services, specializing in USCIS-compliant business plans and concierge EB-5 strategies, creating an overall support team to advise, guide, and travel alongside our clients in every aspect of the business immigration process, whether through our internal team or our strategic partners.

Our unique combination of support and expertise is invaluable for projects seeking a quarterback to coordinate all of the moving parts so that they can attract foreign investor capital and hopeful foreign nationals seeking to enter the United States to make a difference in their lives and the lives of their family members and to make a positive impact on the U.S. economy and society.

For more information, please visit www.ecouncilinc.com or contact us by email at info@ecouncilinc.com or toll-free at 1-866-724-0085. We are here to serve, and it would certainly be our pleasure to be of service to you and your clients and colleagues!

APPENDIX

Visa Tables

The tables on the following pages highlight some of the more prominent elements of many of the business visa types highlighted in this Guide.

Visa Type	E-1	E-2	L-1A	L-1B	H-1B	EB-2	EB-5 Direct	EB-5 Regional Center
Visa Type/ Designation	Non-immigrant (temporary work) Treaty Traders	Non-immigrant (temporary work) Treaty Traders	Non-immigrant (temporary work) Intracompany Transferee Executive or Manager	Non-immigrant (temporary work) Intracompany Transferee Specialized Knowledge	Non-immigrant (temporary work) Specialty Occupations	Employment based immigrant visa (path to citizenship)	Immigrant (path to citizenship)	Immigrant (path to citizenship)
Who can apply?	Must be a national of a treaty country	Must be a national of a treaty country	Must have worked in a managerial or executive capacity abroad for 1 out of the last 3 years – applicant can be from any country	Must have worked in a specialized knowledge capacity abroad for 1 out of the last 3 years – applicant can be from any country	Foreign employee from any country with a job offer from employer willing to sponsor visa and meets educational qualification and requirements for position	Foreign employee, from any country. Must have an advanced degree and/or exceptional ability – "a degree of expertise significantly above that ordinarily encountered in the sciences, arts, or business."	Foreign investor from ANY COUNTRY that meets the investment requirements	Foreign investor from ANY COUNTRY that meets the investment requirements

Visa Type	E-1	E-2	L-1A	L-1B	H-1B	EB-2	EB-5 Direct	EB-5 Regional Center
U.S. Position	Must be coming to the U.S. to engage in substantial trade with the treaty country	Must be coming to direct and control the new U.S. enterprise	Must be coming to the US to work primarily in a managerial or executive capacity	Must be coming to the US to work primarily in a specialized knowledge capacity	Must be coming to the US to fill a specialty occupation position	Job must require an advanced degree and/or foreign employee must demonstrate an exceptional ability in the arts, sciences, or business.	May work as an employee of the NCE or have limited involvement; may work independently of investment	May work independently of subject of investment
Investment Requirements	No specific requirement other than to obtain sufficient premises	Must be "substantial" relative to the capitalization of the U.S. enterprise; enterprise cannot be "marginal"	No specific requirement other than to obtain sufficient premises and adequately capitalize the business (if new)	No specific requirement other than to obtain sufficient premises and adequately capitalize the business (if new)	No specific investment requirements	No specific investment requirements	$1,000,000 or $500,000 in a TEA	$1,000,000 or $500,000 in a TEA
Processing Times	Typically 2-4 weeks, but may be longer depending on the consulate workload. Option to expedite available with additional Premium Processing fee	Generally 1-4 months depending on the consulate. Option for Premium Processing available (15 days or less)	Generally 1-3 months. Option for Premium Processing available (15 days or less)	Same as L-1A	As all cases differ, processing times vary, but it usually takes between 3-6 months for processing. Option to expedite available with additional Premium Processing fee	At least 6 months, but could be years depending on the number of visas available. EB-2 visas qualify for Premium Processing fee to expedite case in 15 days or less.	12-18 months before receiving conditional visa. Another 21-24 months before holder can apply to remove conditions from visa, and roughly 22 months before approval from USCIS (about 5 years in total).	Same as for EB-5 Direct. USCIS does not distinguish between the two. No premium Processing fee available for EB-5 Direct or Regional Center applicants.

FINDING YOUR SILVER LINING

Visa Type	E-1	E-2	L-1A	L-1B	H-1B	EB-2	EB-5 Direct	EB-5 Regional Center
Foreign Company Affiliation	No specific requirement	No specific requirement	Ownership of the foreign and U.S. entities must be substantially similar	Ownership of the foreign and U.S. entities must be substantially similar	No specific requirement	No specific requirement	No specific requirement	No specific requirement
Job Creation Requirement	No specific requirement, but the statute contemplates job creation	Investment must be more than marginal – general expectation that U.S. jobs will be created	Organization must be sufficient to support L-1A visa holder's performing mainly managerial or executive duties	Organization must be sufficient to support L-1A visa holder's performing mainly managerial or executive duties	No specific requirement	No specific requirement	Must create or preserve 10 new, full-time, permanent jobs per investor	Must create or preserve 10 new, full-time, permanent jobs per investor
Green Card Obtainability	Does not lead directly to a green card	Does not lead directly to a green card	Non-immigrant visa with a fast track green card using EB-1 Multinational Manager category (can lead to green card)	Does not lead directly to a green card, but a "dual intent visa'. Can apply for green card without consequences to L-1B visa status	Does not lead directly to a green card, but a "dual intent visa'. Can apply for green card without consequences to H-1B visa status	Filing of I-140 creates eligibility for permanent residency	Filing of I-526 petition creates eligibility for conditional permanent residency Removal of conditions at I-829 stage	Filing of I-526 petition creates eligibility for conditional permanent residency Removal of conditions at I-829 stage

Visa Tables

Visa Type	E-1	E-2	L-1A	L-1B	H-1B	EB-2	EB-5 Direct	EB-5 Regional Center
Dependents	Spouse and unmarried children under 21 can join the principal applicant in E-1 status. Spouse can obtain employment authorization.	Spouse and unmarried children under 21 can join the principal applicant in E-2 status. Spouse can obtain employment authorization.	Spouse and unmarried children under 21 can join the principal applicant in L-2 status. Spouse can obtain employment authorization.	Spouse and unmarried children under 21 can join the principal applicant in L-2 status. Spouse can obtain employment authorization.	Spouse and unmarried children under 21 can join the principal applicant in H-4 status. Spouse can obtain employment authorization.	Spouse and unmarried children under 21 can join the principal applicant in under E-21 and E-22 status, respectfully. Spouse can obtain employment authorization	Spouse and unmarried children under 21 can join the principal applicant in obtaining conditional residency and removal of conditions.	Spouse and unmarried children under 21 can join the principal applicant in obtaining conditional residency and removal of conditions.
Max Initial Stay	5 years	5 years	3 years	3 years	3 years	Indefinitely	2 years, then must apply to remove conditions from visa	2 years, then must apply to remove conditions from visa
Renewability	Yes, can request extensions every 5 years, indefinitely, so long as conditions of visa continue to be met	Yes, indefinitely so long as conditions of visa continue to be met	Yes, can request extensions every 2 years for a maximum stay of 7 years.	Yes, can request extensions every 2 years for a maximum stay of 5 years.	Yes, can request extension after 3 years for a maximum stay of 6 years.	N/A	N/A. If conditions of visa have been met after 2 years, then can apply for permanent residence	N/A. If conditions of visa have been met after 2 years, then can apply for permanent residence

Visa Type	E-1	E-2	L-1A	L-1B	H-1B	EB-2	EB-5 Direct	EB-5 Regional Center
Required Docs	• E-1 specific Business Plan	• E-2 specific Business Plan • 3rd-party CPA financial verification if applying through UK consulate	• L-1A specific Business Plan	• L-1B specific Business Plan			• Matter of Ho compliant Business Plan • Market Study • Private Placement Memo'm (if multiple investors)	• Matter of Ho compliant Business Plan • Market Study • Economic Impact Report • Private Placement Memo'm
Forms	I-129	I-129	I-129	I-129	ETA-9035 and I-129	I-140	I-526 for initial application and two year later I-829 to remove conditions from visa and receive permanent residency/citizenship	I-526 for initial application and two year later I-829 to remove conditions from visa and receive permanent residency/citizenship

Visa Type	E-1	E-2	L-1A	L-1B	H-1B	EB-2	EB-5 (general)
Quotas	None	None	None	None	65,000/year (First, 20,000 with Masters degree or higher are exempt)	40,040/year out of 140,000 total employment based visas per year	Quotas are a hotly-debated EB-5 topic; originally established when EB-5 came about in 1990. Currently, only 10,000 EB-5 visas are available - further divided among projects located in TEA vs non-TEA and urban area. Additional per country quotas also apply. China currently in *retrogression*, meaning that the number of Chinese applicants has extended beyond the country quota and Chinese applicants are in "queue".
Website Sources	https://www.uscis.gov/working-united-states/temporary-workers/e-1-treaty-traders http://ecouncilinc.com/e-1-visa-forgotten-visa/	https://www.uscis.gov/working-united-states/temporary-workers/e-2-treaty-investors http://ecouncilinc.com/business-visa-basics/	https://www.uscis.gov/eir/visa-guide/l-1-intracompany-transferee/l-1-visa http://ecouncilinc.com/business-visa-basics/	https://www.uscis.gov/eir/visa-guide/l-1-intracompany-transferee/l-1-visa http://ecouncilinc.com/business-visa-basics/	https://www.uscis.gov/working-united-states/temporary-workers/h-1b-specialty-occupations-dod-cooperative-research-and-development-project-workers-and-fashion-models	https://www.uscis.gov/working-united-states/permanent-workers/employment-based-immigration-second-preference-eb-2	https://www.uscis.gov/eb-5 http://ecouncilinc.com/quarterback-and-the-eb-5-process/

About e-Council Inc.

e-Council Inc. offers concierge business immigration expertise, specializing in comprehensive project development and investor services. These services range from USCIS-compliant business plans to turnkey EB-5 strategies oriented to those seeking to access the U.S. market through legal immigration and companies seeking alternative capital from foreign investors.

e-Council Inc. creates an overall support team to advise, guide, and travel alongside our clients in every aspect of the business immigration process, whether through our internal team members or our fully-vetted strategic partners. e-Council Inc.'s unique combination of expertise and experience is invaluable for project developers, business owners and foreign nationals seeking a quarterback to coordinate all of the moving parts.

e-Council Inc. helps those seeking to have a positive impact on the U.S. economy and society. Founded on a socially-conscious mission, the e-Council Inc. team know what USCIS wants, and we consistently deliver—our stellar track record is testament to this fact!

The e-Council Inc. team is dedicated to supporting the growth of American companies while creating jobs and helping immigrants seeking the American Dream.

About the Author

Lauren A. Cohen, Esq., a graduate of Osgoode Hall Law School in Toronto, Ontario, is a lawyer licensed in both the United States and Canada. She is an active American Immigration Lawyers Association (AILA) member as well as many other industry and professional groups, and boasts a stellar track record of success. She has firsthand knowledge of the visa process, having become an American citizen in early 2012 following her complex immigration journey to the United States from Canada.

After spending several years working as corporate counsel in various industries while tapping into the field of immigration law, Lauren decided to combine her legal knowledge and business acumen to create *e-Council Inc.*, a virtual company offering concierge turnkey business immigration services ranging from professional business plans to comprehensive project quarterbacking for all types of business visas, with a special focus on EB-5 solutions for direct investment and regional center cases. In response to increasing requests to fix early-stage projects either prior to or after filing, Lauren recently established *The EB-5 Clean-Up Crew™* to assist business owners that have met roadblocks in putting together their EB-5 packages. She also recently developed an *EB-5 Certification and Monitoring Program* reflecting a recognition of a need for improved audit and reporting procedures on the part of issuers to investors. The over-riding goal in all of Lauren's business endeavors is to help her clients achieve their version of the American Dream.

Lauren is an inspired speaker, bringing passion and insight to the multitude of topics on which she speaks, ranging from business immigration to finding balance as a single mom entrepreneur and related topics. Lauren adds great value to events, as she connects with her audience thoroughly through relatable experiences and engaging questions-and-answer sessions. Lauren combines her business savvy, vast experience, and legal skills to educate and inform, while focusing on the human element of running a business and raising a child and finding the elusive balance in life, eliminating the many misconceptions around these complex topics in a way that is customized for each audience.

Lauren is also very community-oriented and a committed philanthropist. She serves on various boards, and recently founded *Find My Silver Lining*, a non-profit whose goal is to inspire single working parents, especially mompreneurs, to persevere through challenging times and focus on the bright side as they strive to lead fulfilling lives. *Find My Silver Lining* will fund *Zevi's Silver Lining*, a program established in affiliation with a local non-profit that is near and dear to Lauren's heart in her beloved father's memory, designed to match children growing up without grandparents with willing grandparents in the community. Lauren's goal is to eventually expand the reach of *Zevi's Silver Linings* to other communities throughout North America.

A regular writer and contributor to books and other media globally, *Finding Your Silver Lining in the Business Immigration Process* is Lauren's first book. Visit her at www.findmysilverlining and www.ecouncilinc.com with more to come soon!

Made in the USA
San Bernardino, CA
19 July 2017